AntiChaos Game Production
– Alignment for Producers & Leads

Build shared intent • Lock decisions fast • Keep scope stable

Gamedev Playbook Series
Volume 1

by Leszek Lisowski

First Edition

ISBN: 978-83-976281-4-4

https://leszeklisowski.com

FOREWORD

Most game projects don't fail because the team is lazy or untalented.

They fail because the project slowly becomes a moving target.

Decisions happen in side channels. Priorities drift. Everyone is "busy," yet nothing feels truly finished. The schedule turns into a negotiation, quality becomes a variable, and heroics quietly replace planning. At some point the team stops asking "What should we do?" and starts asking "What will survive this week?"

This book exists for that moment.

Not to sell you a new methodology. Not to add rituals. Not to drown you in templates. The industry has enough process theater already. What teams need – especially in game development – is a small set of hard, practical rules that reduce chaos without killing creativity.

Because creativity does not require disorder. Creativity requires clear constraints, stable decisions, and fast feedback.

Game development is "software on hard mode." It's cross-discipline work under uncertainty, with tight feedback loops and constant pressure from taste, technology, and time. You can't eliminate uncertainty, but you can stop it from turning into entropy.

That's what AntiChaos Game Production – Alignment for Producers & Leads is about.

It's built around a simple spine:

Align on what "winning" means (pillars, constraints, and explicit non-goals).

Decide with a clear contract (who decides, what inputs are required, and how decisions are recorded).

Ship by protecting momentum (small closures, stable builds, and a plan people can believe).

Along the way, you'll see a recurring theme: most production pain is not a lack of effort but lack of shared reality. People do their best work when they know what matters, what's fixed, what's negotiable, and how change is handled.

This is why the tools in this book are intentionally minimal. The project one-pager. The pillars/constraints/nongoals format. The decision contract starter. The decision log. The change gate. They're not paperwork. They're anchors. If they don't change behavior, they don't belong.

One important note: this book is written from a producer's perspective, but it's not "for producers only." Leads, designers, engineers, artists, and QA will recognize the problems described here, because they live inside the same system. If you're not the formal owner of decisions, you can still use these concepts to push the project toward clarity: by asking for trade-offs, forcing options onto the table, and making "how we decide" explicit.

If you read this book and implement only one thing, make it this:

Stop treating uncertainty as an excuse to delay alignment.

Define what wins. Define what you will not do. Decide openly. Record it. Protect momentum.

That's how you ship without burning the team.

Let's get to work.

CHAPTER 1:
Chaos Patterns & Root Causes
(what chaos looks like in real teams)

I. Chaos symptoms: moving targets, shadow decisions, fake deadlines, heroics/crunch as a strategy

Most teams don't call it "chaos." They call it "fast iteration," "being flexible," "we're still finding the fun," or "just one more push." The problem is that chaos has a very specific smell in production: you can predict the same failure modes weeks before they blow up, because the symptoms repeat across studios, genres, and team sizes.

This section is not about blaming people. It's about naming patterns early enough that you can still steer the project without paying in burnout, rework, and lost credibility.

The first rule of diagnosing chaos

Symptoms are not root causes. They're the smoke. If you attack the smoke (more meetings, more tracking, more pressure), you usually intensify the fire. The goal is to use symptoms as a signal: "we have a decision system problem," "we have an ownership problem," or "we have a planning honesty problem."

You're a producer or a lead. That means you don't get the luxury of "this is above my pay grade." If you can name the symptom clearly, you can usually trigger the right corrective conversation.

Symptom 1: Moving targets

What it looks like in the wild: scope and priorities shift so often that the team stops believing any plan. A feature is "must-have" on Monday, "nice-to-have" on Thursday, and "maybe cut" next Tuesday. The work still happens, but it happens in fragments, with constant context switching and rework.

Why it's dangerous: moving targets don't just waste time. They break *alignment*. When people can't predict what "good" looks like next week, they stop making proactive decisions. They wait. They minimize risk to themselves. They build the safest thing, not the right thing.

Common rationalizations:

- "We're iterative."
- "We're agile."
- "We're responding to feedback."
- "That's gamedev."

Iteration is fine. Randomness isn't. If targets are moving, you need to ask: *Are we moving because we learned something, or because we avoided a hard decision?*

A typical war story (anonymous, but real): A small team keeps rewriting their onboarding because "players are confused." Every two days the solution changes: tutorial popups, then voiceover, then interactive prompts, then a full prologue mission. Nobody can tell you what the current hypothesis is, because the real driver is leadership anxiety about reviews. The target moves not because of evidence, but because fear is steering.

Self-diagnosis questions:

- Can your team describe the top 3 priorities this sprint in the same words?
- When a target changes, is the reason recorded anywhere (even a simple note)?
- Do changes come with trade-offs ("we add X, so we remove Y"), or only with enthusiasm?

If you can't answer these cleanly, you don't have iteration. You have drift.

Symptom 2: Shadow decisions

What it looks like: decisions happen implicitly, in DMs, hallway conversations, side calls, or inside someone's head. The team only discovers the decision when their work is suddenly "wrong." Or worse: different parts of the team believe different decisions were made.

Why it's dangerous: shadow decisions destroy trust. People start acting defensively, because the rules keep changing without warning. Leads stop coordinating because coordination becomes a liability: it's safer to wait for orders than to align.

Shadow decisions also create the illusion of speed. It *feels* faster to decide privately. But the cost comes later as rework, misalignment, and "Why didn't anyone tell me?"

The producer/lead trap: You may even participate in shadow decisions with good intentions: "I'll just confirm this quickly with X so we don't block the team." If the decision changes scope, priorities, quality bar, or meaning of "done," it is no longer "quick." It's a production event.

A typical war story: A lead designer agrees with the creative director in a quick call to "make combat more tactical." No one defines what that means. The next week, one designer adds stamina, another adds cover bonuses, and engineering builds a heavier AI planner. When the director reviews the build, they say "this is not tactical, it's slow." Everyone feels betrayed, even though nobody acted maliciously. The decision was shadowy, so each person filled the gap with their own interpretation.

Self-diagnosis questions:

- How often do people say "I thought we decided…"?
- How often does "approved" mean "approved until I see it"?
- Do you have recurring rework caused by "misunderstanding," not by bugs?

If yes, you don't have a skill problem. You have an explicitness problem.

Symptom 3: Fake deadlines

What it looks like: dates exist, but no one believes them. They're used as pressure tools rather than planning tools. Milestones get missed, then quietly "reframed." The team learns that schedules are political documents, not operational reality.

Why it's dangerous: fake deadlines train people to stop using time as a constraint. If dates are not real, trade-offs are not real. If trade-offs are not real, scope becomes "everything" and quality becomes "eventually."

And fake deadlines don't just hurt delivery. They damage morale because they force people into repeated cycles of hope -> panic -> disappointment -> cynicism.

The most common root cause: deadlines are created from desire, not from capacity. Someone picks a date that *feels* right (publisher beat, event, quarter end), then asks production to "make it happen." Production tries, fails, and loses credibility.

There are legitimate external dates. The "fake" part is when the team pretends the date was derived from a plan, when it wasn't.

Self-diagnosis questions:

- When you announce a deadline, do people quietly roll their eyes?
- Do you regularly hit dates only by crunching, not by planning?
- When a date slips, is the scope reduced, or does everything remain "required"?

Fake deadlines are not harmless. They convert schedule pressure into organizational decay.

Symptom 4: Heroics and crunch as a strategy

What it looks like: the team repeatedly relies on last-minute pushes, weekend saves, and "we'll fix it in polish." Individuals become "heroes" who carry the project. Leadership normalizes this: "That's what it takes."

Why it's dangerous (say it plainly): crunch is a failure mode, not a badge. It is short-term borrowing against long-term capacity. It makes you *feel* productive while increasing defect rates, rework, and staff churn. Over time it also poisons estimation: people start assuming that suffering is part of the plan.

Heroics are seductive because they work... once. The problem is that success through heroics teaches the organization the wrong lesson: "We can always push harder," instead of "We should design the system so we don't need to."

A typical war story: The build is unstable near milestone. A senior engineer stays up two nights, brute-forces fixes, and gets applause. Two months later the same situation repeats, but now everyone expects the same miracle. The engineer becomes a single point of failure, gets resentful, and eventually leaves. The project doesn't just lose a person; it loses the invisible glue that was compensating for systemic problems.

Self-diagnosis questions:

- Are your "best weeks" the ones with the most overtime?
- Do you have key people who are always "the only one who can fix it"?
- Do you celebrate the save, but never fix the condition that required it?

If yes, your production system is rewarding breakdowns.

A simple framework: The Chaos Symptom Map

You want something you can use quickly with leads and producers without turning it into a process festival. Here's the minimal map I'd use:

Think in two axes:

Axis A: Decision visibility

- *Explicit:* decisions are stated, recorded, and shared in a place the team can actually find.
- *Implicit:* decisions exist only in conversations, assumptions, or approvals by vibe.

Axis B: Target stability

- *Stable:* goals change when learning happens, and change includes trade-offs.
- *Volatile:* goals change because of anxiety, politics, or unclear ownership.

Now place your team's reality on the map:

- **Implicit + Volatile** is the chaos pit: moving targets + shadow decisions + fake deadlines + heroics.
- **Explicit + Volatile** is "busy but aligned": you'll still churn, but at least the team knows what changed and why.

- **Implicit + Stable** is "quiet risk": it feels calm until a late reveal causes massive rework.
- **Explicit + Stable** is the goal: you can move fast because people aren't guessing.

This map is useful because it turns vague frustration into a concrete improvement target: *increase explicitness* and/or *reduce volatility*.

What to do as a producer or lead, starting tomorrow

Don't try to "fix chaos." Fix one constraint at a time.

First, pick one symptom you see most often and do one act of explicitness:

- When a target changes, write one sentence: "We changed X because Y, so we're dropping Z."
- When a decision is made, capture: "Decision / Owner / Why / Impact / What changes now."

Second, call out heroics as a risk, not as culture:

- "Thank you for the save. Now we need to remove the condition that made the save necessary."

Third, refuse fake deadlines politely:

- "If this date is fixed, we need a fixed scope. If scope is fixed, we need a flexible date. Which constraint is real?"

That's it. No new ceremonies. No bureaucracy. Just making reality visible and forcing trade-offs to exist in daylight.

If you do those three consistently, chaos doesn't disappear overnight – but it stops compounding. And in production, stopping the compounding is often the difference between shipping and bleeding out.

II. Common sources: no single goal owner, implicit assumptions, no decision contract

If "chaos symptoms" are what you feel day to day, these are the mechanical causes underneath. Not the only ones, but the ones that show up in almost every struggling production regardless of team size or genre.

The important part: these causes don't look dramatic. They look normal. They hide inside "we're all aligned," "we'll figure it out," "everyone knows what we mean," and "let's keep it flexible." That's why they're so expensive: they accumulate quietly, then explode as rework, conflict, missed dates, and crunch.

1) No single goal owner

A goal without an owner is not a goal. It's a wish.

In production terms, "owner" doesn't mean "person who does all the work." It means: one person is accountable for keeping the goal coherent and for forcing trade-offs when reality hits. If a goal has multiple partial owners, it usually has zero real owners. Everyone can influence it, but nobody is responsible for protecting its meaning.

This is where teams accidentally create moving targets. When nobody owns the goal, the goal gets edited by the loudest conversation in the room, the latest feedback, or the most senior person's mood that day.

Here's the mechanical failure:

- A goal exists ("make combat feel tactical," "polish the first hour," "ship by Q3").
- Work starts.
- New information appears (playtest feedback, technical constraints, publisher request).
- Trade-off is required.
- Nobody has the authority/accountability to make the trade-off stick.
- The goal mutates through informal negotiations.
- The team keeps producing output, but alignment decays.

As a producer or lead, your first diagnostic question is brutally simple: *If this goal is threatened, who is obligated to respond?* Not "who cares," not "who has an opinion," but who is expected to take the hit and resolve it.

What does "goal owner" look like in practice? It depends on the type of goal:

- For a product/vision goal, it's usually the game director or equivalent.
- For a milestone goal, it's usually the producer (or delivery owner).
- For a quality bar within a domain (combat, UI, level design), it's typically a lead.

But the key is consistency: one name per goal, and that name can't be "the team."

If you're worried this becomes dictatorship, good. That's the usual fear. But owner ≠ dictator. Owner is the person who must do the hard thing: turn ambiguity into a decision and pay the political cost of trade-offs.

When you don't assign an owner, you still pay that cost. You just pay it later, in rework and attrition.

2) Implicit assumptions

Implicit assumptions are decisions you didn't know you made.

They form when you use words that sound aligned but are actually containers for multiple interpretations. "Tactical." "Responsive." "Cinematic." "Done." "Good enough." "Polish." "Stable." Everyone nods, because nobody wants to be the person who asks "what do you mean by that?" Then everyone builds their own version. Later, you discover you never agreed.

Mechanically, assumptions appear in three places:

First: the **definition of the target**. What exactly are we trying to achieve, and how will we recognize it?

Second: the **constraints**. What cannot be compromised (performance, platform compliance, scope, rating, monetization rules, etc.)?

Third: the **decision rights**. Who can change the target, and when?

Most teams fail on the first one, then get hurt by the second, and explode on the third.

A classic pattern: you have a shared phrase like "we need to polish the first hour." One lead interprets it as UX improvements. Another as visual pass. Engineering interprets it as performance and crash fixes. Production interprets it as cutting content to make the hour tighter. All of these are valid, but they're different goals. Without explicit assumptions, you don't have alignment – you have parallel solo missions.

This is where "shadow decisions" are born. People make local calls based on their private assumptions, because the system didn't give them an explicit shared model. Then those local calls collide.

There are some behaviors that reliably manufacture implicit assumptions. You should call them out directly because they are high-leverage to stop:

- **Approve-by-silence.** "No objections, so we're good." Silence is not consent; it's often fatigue or fear.
- **Drive-by feedback.** A senior person drops an opinion without context or trade-offs, then disappears.
- **Last-minute veto.** Someone who was absent from earlier alignment steps kills the outcome at review time.
- **DM decisions.** People "align quickly" in private, then the team discovers it after the fact.
- **Vibe approvals.** "Looks good" without specifying what "good" means and what would make it "not good."

None of these are character flaws. They're predictable outcomes of a system that doesn't force explicitness.

3) No decision contract

A decision contract is the minimum set of rules that makes decisions real. Without it, you don't have "decision-making." You have an ongoing negotiation with random enforcement.

Most teams don't intentionally avoid a decision contract. They just never formalize what they already believe. And because it's not formal, it fails under stress – exactly when you need it most.

A decision contract answers three practical questions:

1. What kinds of decisions exist, and which ones require explicit visibility?
2. Who owns each decision type (final call), and who must be consulted?
3. What artifact makes a decision "real" and prevents backtracking?

You don't need RACI/DACI terminology to do this. You need a tiny, repeatable protocol that prevents "we thought we decided" situations.

Here's the core mechanic: decisions must have a **definition**, an **owner**, and a **commit signal**.

If any of these are missing, the decision is soft. Soft decisions are the silent tax in gamedev. They look like progress until the moment you try to ship.

Mini decision contract template (simple, usable)

Use this as a lightweight text block you can paste into whatever your team uses (doc, task, chat thread). The format matters less than the habit.

Decision: (one sentence, unambiguous)
Owner: (one person, final call)
Context: (why we're deciding this now)
Options considered: (2–3 short bullets, not exhaustive)
Chosen option + trade-off: (what we pick and what we're not doing)
Constraints: (non-negotiables: performance, platform, time, rating, etc.)
Impact: (what changes in backlog / scope / pipeline)
Commit signal: (what makes it real: "added to sprint," "spec updated," "branch created," "task list approved")
Revisit rule: (when can it be reopened, and by whom)

That last line is the one teams skip. It's also the one that prevents chaos. If every decision can be reopened at any time by anyone, you don't have decisions – you have suggestions.

A healthy revisit rule sounds like: "Reopen only if new evidence appears (playtest data, technical blocker, market constraint), and it must go through the owner."

This doesn't reduce creativity. It reduces thrash.

How these three sources interact

No goal owner means nobody protects the target. Implicit assumptions fill the vacuum. No decision contract means the assumptions never get tested and locked. The result is predictable: moving targets, shadow decisions, fake deadlines, and heroics.

As a producer or lead, you don't fix this by "being stricter" or "tracking harder." You fix it by making three things explicit: ownership, assumptions, and decision reality.

If you do only one thing from this section, do this: pick one key goal currently "in the air," name a single owner, and capture the next decision about it using the mini template above. That alone will surface where your system is leaking alignment.

III. Why gamedev is vulnerable: content dependencies, iteration, build feedback loops, "direction" pressure

If you've worked in "normal" software and then moved into game development, you've probably had this moment: "Why does everything here feel harder than it should be?" Not because people are less competent. Not because tools are worse. Because the product itself is structurally hostile to clean planning.

Gamedev is vulnerable to chaos by design. It's a field where the value of the product is emergent, where quality is subjective until it suddenly isn't, and where progress is often invisible until a build exists. That combination creates a perfect environment for moving targets, shadow decisions, fake deadlines, and heroics – unless you deliberately build anti-chaos constraints.

Below are four pressure sources that make gamedev uniquely prone to production entropy. If you recognize them as "physics," not "culture," you can stop blaming people and start designing a system that survives them.

1) Content dependencies: everything is coupled to everything

In many software products, you can build features with relatively clean interfaces. Data models, APIs, and user flows can be separated. Teams can work in parallel with contracts that are mostly stable.

Games are different. "Content" is not just decoration. Content *is the product*. And content has dependencies in multiple directions: design depends on content, content depends on tech, tech depends on design, and all of it depends on performance constraints that can invalidate work late.

A character ability isn't just a code change. It's animation, VFX, UI, sound, tuning, AI responses, tutorials, localization strings, save compatibility, controller mapping, and sometimes level design changes. You can ship a SaaS feature with a "good enough" UI and improve later. In many games, "good enough later" either breaks immersion or creates a quality mismatch that players notice instantly.

This is why gamedev teams underestimate the cost of change. They see "small change" at the design surface, but they don't see the dependency blast radius underneath.

Dependency pressure produces chaos in two ways.

First, it punishes partial work. A half-finished feature isn't valuable; it's a liability that steals attention during integration.

Second, it creates hidden critical paths. Art can't finalize because design is unstable. Design can't finalize because playtests require a build. The build can't stabilize because content keeps changing. Everyone is "waiting" while also being "busy."

If you want a simple diagnostic: when a game team says "we're blocked," it's often not a single blocker. It's a dependency knot.

2) Iteration: you don't know the truth until you can play it

Iteration is a virtue in game development. It's also a chaos engine.

In software, you can validate many requirements with logic, specs, and unit tests. In games, the core question is experiential: "Is this fun?" "Does this feel right?" "Is this readable?" "Is the pacing correct?" You cannot fully answer that in a document. You need to feel it, and that requires a playable slice.

That creates a structural problem: you often have to invest a meaningful amount of work before you can learn whether the direction is correct. And once you learn, you might have to throw away part of that investment.

This is where teams accidentally turn "iteration" into "thrash." The line between the two is not how many times you change something. It's whether each change is driven by a clear hypothesis and a controlled test, or by anxiety and taste battles.

Games also iterate across multiple dimensions at once. You can't just "iterate on combat" while keeping everything else fixed, because combat feel depends on camera, input latency, animation timing, readability, enemy design, audio feedback, and difficulty curve. Each iteration touches a web of dependencies.

So iteration pressure is real. The anti-chaos move is not to reduce iteration. It's to give iteration boundaries: clear hypotheses, timeboxed experiments, and protection of what is already stable.

3) Build feedback loops: reality arrives late, and it arrives with interest

A build is the ultimate truth source. It's also expensive, slow, and emotionally loaded.

In many teams, the build becomes a feedback bottleneck. You can have a thousand tasks "in progress," but until the build compiles, runs, and is testable, you don't actually know what you've made. That delays learning, which increases risk, which increases pressure, which increases chaos behaviors.

Build feedback loops create a particularly nasty cycle:

You delay integration because "it's not ready."
Because integration is delayed, issues surface late.
Because issues surface late, the fix window shrinks.
Because the fix window shrinks, people crunch.
Because people crunch, quality drops.
Because quality drops, the build becomes unstable.
Because the build is unstable, you delay integration even more.

This is why "heroics" feel necessary near milestones. The build is screaming truths you ignored for weeks.

If you've ever heard "we'll stabilize later," you've seen this loop. "Later" is almost always more expensive because the dependency graph has grown, more work is stacked on top, and the team has lost context.

Compared to many IT products, games are also more sensitive to non-functional issues that are hard to predict: performance spikes, memory pressure, content streaming, platform quirks, certification constraints. You can build a feature that is logically correct and still unshippable because it drops frames in a way that ruins feel. That's build feedback loop pressure in its purest form: the experience is the spec, and the build is the only honest measure.

4) "Direction" pressure: creative intent becomes identity, and identity resists trade-offs

In most software, direction is usually expressed as goals and constraints: solve a user problem, hit an SLA, reduce churn, comply with regulation. There can be strong opinions, but the success criteria are usually more legible.

In games, direction is not just a goal. It's often the identity of the project and the identity of the creative leads. That creates a unique kind of pressure: any compromise can feel like betrayal.

Direction pressure has an organizational layer and a psychological layer.

Organizationally, "direction" often sits in a role that has high authority but low bandwidth. A game director or creative owner cannot be in every discussion. So the team fills the gaps with assumptions, and later gets corrected through drive-by feedback or last-minute veto. That creates shadow decisions and rework even when everyone is acting in good faith.

Psychologically, direction is tied to taste and fear. Fear of losing what makes the game special. Fear of shipping something average. Fear of being judged. That fear doesn't show up as "I'm scared." It shows up as endless revisions, perfectionism, late pivots, and refusal to cut "signature" features.

Direction pressure also amplifies fake deadlines. People want the external date and the internal dream simultaneously. When reality forces trade-offs, the team often chooses denial: keep the date, keep the scope, and solve the contradiction with heroics.

This is why gamedev needs decision discipline more than many other fields. Not because game teams are worse. Because direction is more subjective, more identity-loaded, and more dependent on late feedback.

A compact model: four chaos forces

If you want one mental model to keep in your head, it's this: gamedev chaos tends to come from four forces that multiply each other.

Dependencies make change expensive.
Iteration makes change necessary.

Build loops make truth arrive late.
Direction pressure makes trade-offs emotionally and politically hard.

When these forces are unmanaged, your production becomes an anxiety machine. People react instead of decide.

The goal of an anti-chaos production system is not to eliminate these forces. You can't. They're the nature of the medium. The goal is to keep them from compounding into systemic failure.

That typically means: make ownership explicit, force trade-offs into daylight, stabilize the build earlier than feels comfortable, and translate "direction" into concrete, testable statements instead of vibe.

This is also why "just do what software does" rarely works. You can import tools and ceremonies, but if you don't address these four forces, you'll end up with the worst of both worlds: heavy process and the same chaos symptoms.

Gamedev doesn't need more tracking. It needs a decision system that's strong enough to survive its own physics.

IV. How to tell "creative turbulence" from destructive chaos (signals and thresholds)

Every healthy game goes through turbulence. If you try to remove all turbulence, you'll ship something safe, bland, and under-tested. The goal is not calm. The goal is *controlled instability*: you're allowed to shake the box, but you don't let the box fall apart.

Destructive chaos looks similar from the outside – lots of movement, lots of opinions, lots of change – but it has a different internal signature. Turbulence produces learning and convergence. Chaos produces exhaustion and divergence.

As a producer or lead, you need a practical way to tell the difference early, before the team pays for it in rework and burnout. You won't get perfect certainty. But you can get good enough signals and clear thresholds to trigger intervention.

The core distinction: convergence vs. divergence

Creative turbulence is change that *narrows* the solution space over time. Even if you try five variants, you end up with fewer unknowns and more clarity.

Destructive chaos is change that *expands* the solution space. Every iteration adds more questions than answers. Decisions don't become stronger; they become softer. People stop trusting plans because plans don't survive contact with leadership mood swings or build instability.

If you want one sentence to anchor on:

Turbulence turns uncertainty into knowledge. Chaos turns uncertainty into anxiety.

Signal set 1: what happens to the "why"

In creative turbulence, the "why" becomes sharper. You might disagree, but you can articulate the reason behind changes.

In chaos, the "why" degrades into vibes and authority. People can tell you what changed, but not why it changed, and not what trade-off was accepted.

Ask two questions after any meaningful change:

- Why did we change this now?
- What are we *not* doing because of this change?

If the answers are clear and repeatable, you're probably in turbulence. If the answers are vague, shifting, or politically avoided, you're drifting into chaos.

A subtle but telling sign: in turbulence, teams argue about the game. In chaos, teams argue about communication and fairness. "Why wasn't I told?" "Who approved this?" "Why did we redo this again?" Those are governance symptoms, not creative ones.

Signal set 2: the decision footprint

Creative turbulence still leaves a footprint. Decisions are visible enough that the team can orient themselves, even if they don't love the outcome.

Chaos has a "no footprint" pattern. Decisions happen, but they don't exist anywhere. That's when you get "I thought we decided…" as a weekly ritual.

You don't need bureaucracy to fix this. You need a minimum decision trace. If you can't point to a simple record of what was decided, by whom, and what it impacts, you've crossed into chaos territory.

This is also where last-minute veto becomes your red flag. Turbulence can include reversals, but reversals are triggered by new evidence. Chaos reversals are triggered by late taste reactions or power dynamics.

Signal set 3: build health as the hard boundary

This is the one most teams ignore because it's uncomfortable: build stability is not "a technical detail." It's the boundary between learning and thrash.

If your build is unstable, you are not iterating – you are guessing. And guessing amplifies both creative uncertainty and production pressure.

Creative turbulence can happen on top of a stable build. You can change direction and still keep the system testable.

Destructive chaos almost always correlates with build decay:

- Integration is delayed because "it's not ready."
- QA becomes reactive and overwhelmed.
- Bugs become noise, not signal.
- People avoid touching systems because everything is fragile.
- The team stops trusting the build, so feedback slows down.
- Slower feedback makes decisions weaker, which increases chaotic change.

The threshold here is qualitative but sharp: **if the team cannot reliably get feedback from a build on the things they're changing, you're past turbulence and into chaos.**

A practical heuristic: if you have to ask "which build should I test?" too often, your feedback loop is broken. If you have a "special person" who knows how to make builds work, your project is being held together by heroics, not process.

Signal set 4: rework pattern – targeted vs. random

Rework is not automatically bad. In early stages, rework is expected. What matters is the pattern.

Creative turbulence produces *targeted* rework. You rework specific things because you learned something specific. The team can say: "We're redoing X because we learned Y, and we'll know it worked if Z."

Destructive chaos produces *random* rework. People redo things because the target moved or because someone reacted late. The rework doesn't create closure; it creates more open loops.

Watch for this smell: rework that keeps changing the same layer (UI polish, VFX pass, tuning) without improving core understanding. It's busywork driven by discomfort, not learning.

Another smell: rework that invalidates work across disciplines without warning. That usually means you don't have a decision contract and you don't have a goal owner. People are iterating locally while the global direction is unstable.

Signal set 5: team energy and planning realism

In turbulence, the team is tired sometimes, but motivated. There is a sense that effort converts into progress. People might say "we're still figuring it out," but they can also say "we're closer than last month."

In chaos, effort stops converting into progress. People still work hard, but morale decays because they can't see convergence. You start hearing:

- "What's the point?"
- "Let's wait until they decide."
- "It'll change again anyway."
- "Just do it, we'll redo later."

Producers and leads should treat that language as a production metric. It's not "attitude." It's information: the system is producing learned helplessness.

Planning realism is similar. In turbulence, plans are imperfect but respected; adjustments come with trade-offs. In chaos, plans are theater. Deadlines are fake, and everyone knows.

Thresholds you can use without numbers

Qualitative thresholds. Here are the ones that actually work in day-to-day leadership.

You are still in creative turbulence if:

- Changes are tied to explicit learning (playtest, performance, clear feedback), not to mood.
- The number of open questions is shrinking, even if slowly.
- Decisions leave a trace that prevents "surprise reversals."
- The build remains usable as a feedback instrument.
- Trade-offs are spoken out loud.

You have crossed into destructive chaos if any of these become true consistently:

- The build is too unstable to validate the changes you're making.
- Rework is driven by late veto or "drive-by feedback," not by new evidence.

- Teams can't describe the current priorities in the same words.
- Decisions are routinely discovered after the fact.
- Heroics are required to maintain basic momentum.

That last one is worth repeating: **if heroics are required for normal operation, you are in chaos.** Crunch is not "just a busy period." It is the system telling you it cannot handle its own uncertainty.

A simple stoplight system (adaptable)

This is intentionally lightweight. You can use it in a weekly, in a lead sync, or even in a private self-check. The point is not the colors. The point is triggering the right conversation early.

Green (turbulence):
You're iterating, but you can explain why. The build is testable. Changes converge. Rework is targeted.

Yellow (edge):
You're still learning, but feedback loops are slowing down. Build stability is wobbling. Decisions are getting softer. Rework is spreading across disciplines. People start hedging.

Yellow is not a failure. Yellow is a warning to add constraints. You tighten decision traces, you freeze certain layers (e.g., content intake), you protect build health. You don't "push harder." You stabilize the system.

Red (chaos):
Build feedback is unreliable. Decisions reverse late. Rework is random. Heroics are normalized. The team doesn't trust plans.

Red requires intervention, not encouragement. You stop pretending. You reduce scope. You define owners. You lock decision rules. You restore build stability as priority zero. Otherwise you're just spending people.

You can adapt this system by choosing your own "gate checks." The most important one, in my opinion, is the build gate. Because if the build is sick, everything else becomes opinion wars.

What to do when you detect the transition

This section isn't about fixing it yet, but one tactical move matters immediately: **don't argue about whether it's chaos. Argue about what signal you're seeing.**

Producers and leads often lose weeks fighting over interpretation. Use objective-ish signals: build stability, decision trace, trade-offs, rework pattern.

When someone says "we're just being creative," you can respond calmly: "Great. Show me the learning and show me the convergence. If we can't validate in the build and we can't explain the trade-offs, that's not creativity. That's thrash."

That's direct, respectful, and accurate.

And it sets the tone for the rest of this book: anti-chaos isn't anti-creativity. It's pro-shipping.

V. The most common lies we tell ourselves: "we'll define it later," "we'll do it in polish," "it's just a small change."

These are not innocent phrases. They are production debt instruments.

They show up in every studio, even good ones, because they feel reasonable in the moment. They help you move forward when you're tired, uncertain, or under pressure. The problem is that they don't remove uncertainty. They postpone it. And postponed uncertainty doesn't stay the same size. It grows, collects interest, and eventually shows up as rework, conflict, and crunch.

When I call them "lies," I don't mean people are malicious. I mean the statement is mechanically false in game production. The cost exists whether you acknowledge it or not.

Lie #1: "We'll define it later"

What you usually mean is: "We don't agree yet, but we don't want to block work."

This is the most common way teams accidentally create moving targets and shadow decisions. The team starts building in parallel based on private interpretations. Later, "defining it" becomes painful because now you're not defining an idea – you're invalidating real work. So definition gets delayed again. Eventually you hit a milestone, panic, and define it under duress. That's where bad decisions get locked in, because the schedule is now doing the deciding.

Gamedev makes this lie especially seductive because definition often requires play. You can't fully define "feel" on paper. So people tell themselves "later" is logical. The failure is assuming definition can remain ambiguous while production stays efficient.

Here's the mechanical truth: if you don't define the target, the team will define it for you – implicitly, inconsistently, and expensively.

The antidote is not "define everything up front." That's impossible. The antidote is to define *enough* to protect alignment and to make iteration meaningful.

A practical counter-move: when someone says "we'll define it later," ask for a minimal definition now. Not a perfect one. A *usable* one.

What does "usable" look like? It can be as simple as:

- a one-sentence intention ("This feature exists to make X decision more interesting"),
- a constraint ("Must work on controller; must not add new tutorial steps"),
- and one success/failure signal ("We'll know it works if new players do Y within 30 seconds").

That's not bureaucracy. That's preventing the team from building three different versions of "later."

Another counter-move: define the *revisit rule* now. Later is only safe if you also say: "We revisit after build X, with playtest Y, and the owner is Z." If you can't name when and how you'll define it later, you're not postponing. You're avoiding.

Lie #2: "We'll do it in polish"

Polish is the graveyard where teams bury unfinished thinking.

The word "polish" has a legitimate meaning: improving readability, pacing, feedback, presentation, and feel once the underlying structure is stable. The lie is using "polish" as a placeholder for unresolved design, missing content, technical debt, and quality risks that are not actually polish tasks.

The reason this lie is so common is psychological. It gives comfort. It's a way to say "we know it's not good, but we'll fix it later" without confronting what "fix" really means. It also protects direction pressure: you don't have to admit the current implementation might be structurally wrong.

But in real production, late polish time is small, fragile, and constantly attacked by reality: bugs, integration issues, performance problems, platform requirements, and certification. If you treat polish as a safety net for fundamental problems, you are betting the project on a phase that rarely exists in the form you imagine.

Here's the mechanical truth: polish can improve what is already coherent. It cannot rescue what is incomplete or misaligned.

A useful way to separate real polish from fake polish is to ask: "Does this require changing structure, or only improving signal?"

If you need to add systems, redesign flows, create new content, redo animations, or change core tuning assumptions, that's not polish. That's production work, with production risk.

Producers and leads should treat "we'll do it in polish" as a trigger to classify the work:

- Is this a **readability/feedback** improvement (true polish)?
- Is this a **missing piece** that blocks correct evaluation (not polish)?
- Is this a **quality bar** decision we've avoided (not polish)?
- Is this **technical stability** work disguised as polish (definitely not polish)?

The counter-move is to make "polish" conditional on a stable foundation. The foundation is usually: stable build, stable scope for core loop, stable content intake for critical paths. If those aren't true, you're not approaching polish – you're approaching crunch.

A second counter-move: rename the work. Literally. Words shape behavior. If a task is "polish," it gets deprioritized until late. If it's "core loop readability gate" or "onboarding clarity fix," it gets treated as a structural requirement. Teams often hide real work under the label "polish" because it feels less threatening. Don't let language sabotage you.

Lie #3: "It's just a small change"

This one kills schedules quietly.

In games, "small" is rarely about the size of the change in one discipline. It's about the number of dependencies it touches and the uncertainty it introduces. A small code change can cause a cascade of animation updates, UI re-layouts, tutorial changes, balance retuning, VFX rework, QA retesting, and performance revalidation. A small art change can break readability. A small design tweak can invalidate a level's pacing.

The lie persists because humans are bad at seeing dependency graphs in their heads. Also because calling it "small" is socially convenient. It avoids confrontation. It sounds like you're being reasonable.

Here's the mechanical truth: there are no small changes, only changes with small *blast radius*. And you don't know the blast radius unless you ask.

So the counter-move is not to shut down changes. It's to force a fast blast-radius check before you say yes.

You can do this without turning it into bureaucracy by using a simple mental filter:

- What disciplines does this touch?
- What needs retesting because of it?
- What is the failure mode if we don't do it?
- What do we stop doing to make room?

If the change touches more than one discipline or requires broad retesting, it's not "small." It might still be worth it, but it's not small. Name it honestly.

There's another hidden risk here: "small changes" accumulate. One small change per day is a slow-moving pivot. If you allow lots of small changes without trade-offs, you're not iterating. You're leaking capacity.

A producer's role is to turn "small" into "priced." Not priced in money – priced in time, attention, and risk.

Why these lies show up under pressure

These lies tend to spike when direction pressure rises and when build feedback loops are weak. When you can't validate fast, you can't close decisions, so you postpone definition. When the build is unstable, you can't confidently improve quality, so you push it into "polish." When you're behind schedule, you try to sneak improvements in as "small changes," because admitting the real cost would force trade-offs you don't want to fight for.

In other words: these lies are coping mechanisms for a weak decision system.

A simple shared counter-language

You don't need to shame people. You need shared phrases that break the spell.

When someone says "we'll define it later," you can respond calmly:
"Define the minimum now: intent, constraint, and one success signal. Then we can iterate."

When someone says "we'll do it in polish," you can respond:

"Is this signal improvement or structural change? If it's structural, it's not polish. Let's classify it."

When someone says "it's just a small change," you can respond:
"Let's do a 2-minute blast-radius check. If it crosses disciplines or re-testing, we price it and trade it."

These are not clever tricks. They are anti-chaos habits. They keep the team honest about uncertainty, which is the only way you get to alignment, real decisions, and shipping without burning people.

And that's the theme of this entire series: you can't eliminate uncertainty in gamedev. But you can stop lying to yourself about what uncertainty costs.

VI. Hidden costs: rework, loss of trust in plans, quality drop, churn

Chaos is rarely paid for upfront. That's why teams tolerate it. The invoices arrive later, in forms that are easy to misattribute: "We're just unlucky," "This project is cursed," "The market is tough," "People are unprofessional," "The engine is fighting us."

No. Most of the time, you're paying interest on unmanaged uncertainty.

The hidden costs below are the real reason chaotic teams burn out even when they "work hard" and even when the game has potential. If you're a producer or a lead, you can't afford to treat these as soft, emotional side effects. They are production mechanics. They hit schedule, budget, quality, and ultimately your ability to ship.

Rework: the tax you pay when decisions aren't real

Rework is not the same as iteration. Iteration is a controlled loop: you try something, you learn, you converge. Rework is what happens when the target moved or was never defined, when feedback arrived too late, or when a late veto invalidated finished work.

The cost of rework is not just "doing the task twice." It includes context rebuilding, integration overhead, retesting, and lost momentum. Rework also multiplies across disciplines because games are coupled systems. A "small" change in direction can invalidate animation sets, VFX, UI layout, tutorial logic, tuning, and level pacing.

Here's a pattern you've seen: a feature ships to a playable state, then gets "revisited" three times. Each revisit starts with "it's just a tweak," and ends with "why is this still not right?" The real reason is usually that the team never agreed on what "right" means, and the build feedback loop was too slow to close the decision early.

From a business perspective, rework destroys your burn efficiency. You might spend the same monthly payroll, but you get less net progress. That shortens runway without improving the product.

Publishers and external partners feel this too. If your milestone deliveries keep changing shape, you lose credibility. Even when the game is good, the relationship becomes risk management instead of partnership. You start getting more oversight, more approvals, more reporting. That's not because they're evil. It's because you taught them you can't predict your own output.

Loss of trust in plans: when schedules become theater

This is one of the most damaging costs, and it's invisible until it's too late. When a team stops trusting plans, planning stops working as a coordination tool. People stop aligning their work around milestones because milestones don't mean anything. They start optimizing locally: "I'll just finish my piece," "I'll wait for clarity," "I'll avoid risky tasks," "I'll keep options open." That looks reasonable at the individual level, but it destroys the project at the system level.

A plan you don't believe is not a plan. It's performance.

Once planning becomes theater, you get predictable secondary effects:

- estimates become lies, because nobody wants to be blamed for reality;
- commitments are replaced by vague intentions;
- priorities change through politics instead of trade-offs;
- "alignment" becomes repetition of slogans, not shared understanding.

This is also where fake deadlines become dangerous. Teams don't just miss them. They stop using time as a constraint. When time is no longer a constraint, scope becomes fantasy and quality becomes undefined. That's how you end up with crunch as a strategy: you keep pretending the date is real and pay the difference in human cost.

In strong teams, a plan is not a promise. It's a tool for coordinating decisions. Chaos destroys the tool by making it untrusted.

Quality drop: not a gradual slide, a systemic collapse

Quality drop in chaotic production is not usually "we didn't polish enough." It's structural.

When people are constantly redoing work, they stop doing it well. Not because they don't care, but because they're protecting themselves from wasted effort. The team becomes conservative: minimal effort, minimal risk, minimal creativity. That's one form of quality drop.

The other form is rushed integration. Late changes collide, builds become unstable, QA loses signal in noise, and defects flood in. You start triaging symptoms instead of improving the game. The product becomes fragile: every fix causes two new problems because the system is under-tested and the team is exhausted.

This is where your build feedback loop matters. A stable build is a quality instrument. An unstable build is a quality destroyer. If the team cannot reliably test and validate changes, quality becomes a matter of hope. Hope is not a production strategy.

From a market perspective, quality drop compounds. A weak launch build doesn't just create bugs – it creates reviews, refunds, and reputation damage. On platforms like Steam, early sentiment can anchor future conversion. On consoles, certification issues can delay releases and force costly resubmissions. Even in early access, quality chaos can poison community trust: players stop believing you'll fix things, and they stop giving useful feedback.

The brutal truth: many games don't fail because they lacked talent. They fail because chaos forced them to ship a version that made the market conclude "this studio can't deliver."

Churn: the bill comes due in people

"Churn" is not just resignation. It's also burnout, quiet quitting, and the slow erosion of discretionary effort.

In chaotic production, the best people often leave first. Not because they're weak, but because they have options and they can see the trajectory. They don't want to spend another year in a system that rewards heroics and punishes clarity.

When churn hits, the cost isn't just recruitment. It's knowledge loss and increased risk. Games are complex. They carry huge amounts of tacit context: why something was done, what was tried, what broke last time, what the real constraints are. When someone leaves, you don't just lose output – you lose memory. That creates more rework, which creates more chaos, which drives more churn. It's a feedback loop.

Even without resignations, you can lose your team psychologically. People disengage. They stop fighting for quality. They stop proposing improvements. They stop calling out risks because calling out risks never changes anything. That's quiet quitting, and it's lethal because it looks like "everything is fine" right until the moment nothing moves.

You can also see churn risk through behavior: constant overtime by a few "heroes," increasing sick days, sudden drops in communication, rising sarcasm, more defensive language. Those are not "attitude problems." They're system alarms.

The leadership behaviors that amplify hidden costs

It is important to allow yourself to have some clear anti-patterns. Here they are, stated plainly.

If leaders regularly do drive-by feedback, last-minute veto, approve-by-silence, and DM decisions, they are manufacturing rework and killing trust. They might believe they're "protecting direction." What they're actually doing is destabilizing the system that must deliver direction.

If producers accept fake deadlines without trading scope, they are trading team health and quality for the illusion of control.

If leads tolerate "small changes" without blast-radius checks, they are slowly converting iteration into thrash.

None of this requires bad intentions. But good intentions do not pay the bill. Mechanics do.

How these hidden costs connect

These costs are not separate. They cascade.

Rework makes plans inaccurate.
Inaccurate plans destroy trust.
Loss of trust drives local optimization and disengagement.
Disengagement and pressure reduce quality.
Quality problems create more rework and more pressure.

Pressure and heroics drive churn.
Churn destroys continuity, increasing rework again.

If you've ever felt like a project was stuck in a spiral, this is why. The system is amplifying itself.

A short mirror diagnosis (for producers and leads)

You don't need metrics to spot this. Answer these honestly.

Do you regularly redo work because of late feedback or unclear targets, not because of new evidence?

Do people treat schedules as theater – something to present, not something to trust?
Is build stability getting worse as you get closer to milestones, instead of better?
Are your best people carrying disproportionate load, and is that becoming "normal"?
Do you hear "it'll change anyway" or "let's wait until they decide" more often than you'd like?

Have you lost someone recently and realized the real loss was not headcount, but project memory?

If you answered "yes" to multiple questions, you're not just dealing with stress. You're paying chaos interest.

The good news is that these costs are not mysterious. They're predictable. Which means they're fixable – if you stop treating them as side effects and start treating them as system outputs.

VII. Mini-audit: a quick 5-question project test – is this still adaptation, or already entropy?

You don't need a dashboard to tell if a project is adapting or decaying. You need five honest questions asked on a regular cadence, with the discipline to treat the answers as signals – not as debate topics.

This mini-audit is designed for producers and leads. Use it weekly (lead sync), at the end of a sprint, or any time you feel that "we're busy but not moving." It's intentionally lightweight: five questions, each one targeting a common entropy leak. The goal is not to score people. The goal is to detect when your system is starting to compound chaos.

The output should be simple: "We're still adapting" or "We're in entropy territory." Then you pick one corrective action, not ten.

How to use it

Answer each question with one of three states: **Yes**, **Mostly**, or **No**. You don't need to turn that into a numeric score unless you want to. But you do need to treat "No" as a red flag and "Mostly" as yellow.

A useful threshold is practical:

If you have **two or more "No" answers**, you're not just adapting – you're leaking alignment and predictability. If you have **one "No" plus multiple "Mostly,"** you're on the edge.

Now the questions.

1) Do we have a single, current "direction" statement the team would repeat the same way?

This is not about having a vision document. It's about whether the project has a clear and current north star that prevents random changes from being justified as "direction."

If you ask three people (producer, design lead, tech lead) "what are we optimizing for right now?" and you get three different answers, you are not aligned. You are improvising.

Adaptation means the direction can evolve, but it evolves explicitly. Entropy means the direction drifts through vibes, mood, and late feedback.

If the answer is "Mostly," ask yourself what's missing: is it the intent, the target audience, the experience goal, or the quality bar?

2) When priorities change, do we state the trade-off out loud?

This is the fastest test of whether you're making real decisions or just stacking more work.

A healthy change sounds like: "We're adding X because we learned Y, so we're dropping Z."

An entropy change sounds like: "We need X now," with no removal, no cost, and no owner.

If you can't name what stopped being important, your "priorities" are marketing language. This is one of the core mechanisms behind rework and crunch. You keep adding, nothing is removed, and the schedule silently turns into a debt collector.

If the answer is "No," you don't have a prioritization problem. You have a trade-off avoidance problem.

3) Can we get reliable feedback from the build on what we're changing this week?

This is the difference between iteration and guessing.

If your build is unstable, integration is delayed, or testing is inconsistent, you can't close loops. You can't learn fast enough. That turns creative work into opinion wars and forces late panic decisions.

You don't need perfection. You need reliability. The question is not "is the build flawless?" The question is "can we validate the changes we're making without fighting the build?"

A "Mostly" here is often a warning. "Mostly" usually means certain people know how to get a working build, or QA is compensating with manual workarounds, or you have pockets of stability but no overall trust.

If the answer is "No," your project is operating without an instrument panel. Expect entropy to accelerate.

4) Are decisions visible enough that nobody is surprised by them?

You don't need a heavy process. You need a minimum decision trace.

If people keep discovering decisions after the fact – through changed tasks, rejected work, or sudden pivots – your decision system is leaking. That leak creates shadow decisions, rework, and resentment. Even good people start to disengage because they can't trust the ground under them.

The test is simple: do you hear "I thought we decided..." or "when did that change?" often?

If you answer "Mostly," you're likely in a dangerous middle state: you're communicating some things, but critical decisions still happen privately or implicitly.

Entropy loves this state because it looks functional until it collapses at a milestone.

5) Are we protecting team capacity, or are we normalizing heroics?

If heroics are required for normal operation, you are not adapting. You are compensating.

This question is not a moral stance. It's a production mechanic. Over time, chronic overtime reduces quality, increases defect rates, and trains the organization to rely on last-minute miracles. It also creates single points of failure, where the "hero" becomes the glue holding the project together – until they burn out or leave.

The test is not "did we crunch once." It's whether you're treating crunch as a planned tool.

If you say "Mostly," you're probably doing quiet normalization: you don't say "crunch," but you assume evenings and weekends are available whenever the build goes red.

That's entropy. It's just slow-motion.

Interpreting results without overthinking

If you answered **Yes** to most questions, you're likely in adaptation. You still have uncertainty, but your system is converting it into learning.

If you hit **two or more No**, you're in entropy territory. You don't need more tracking. You need one constraint that stops the leak.

If you got **one No and several Mostly**, treat it as a warning: you're stable enough to recover cheaply, but only if you act now.

What to do when the audit says "entropy"

Pick one action based on the weakest area. Don't do a broad "process overhaul." That usually creates more chaos.

If direction is unclear: compress it into a single paragraph and align leads on the exact wording. Then freeze it for a short window so the team can execute without whiplash.

If trade-offs aren't explicit: enforce a rule that any new priority must name what it replaces. If nothing can be replaced, it's not a priority – it's a wish.

If build feedback is unreliable: make build stability a first-class deliverable for a short window. Cut scope before you cut sleep. Stabilizing late is always more expensive.

If decisions are invisible: introduce a tiny decision log using the mini template from earlier. Decisions that change scope, priorities, or quality bar must leave a trace. No trace, no decision.

If heroics are normalized: stop celebrating saves as strategy. Thank the effort, then remove the condition that required it. Start by identifying the top two recurring "emergency causes" and fixing those, not by asking for more sacrifice.

The point of this audit is not to prove you're failing. It's to give you permission to intervene early, while the fixes are still cheap.

In the next sections, we'll turn these signals into a decision system that keeps the project aligned, makes trade-offs real, and protects your ability to ship without burning the team.

CHAPTER 2: Alignment That Holds (pillars, constraints, nongoals)

I. Operational alignment defined: not "everyone agrees," but "everyone knows what wins"

Most teams think alignment means agreement. It doesn't.

Agreement is a mood. Alignment is an operating system.

You can have a team that "agrees" in meetings and still ships incoherent work, because each person is optimizing for a different definition of success. You can also have a team that disagrees loudly and still ships well, because despite the conflict they share the same win conditions. They argue inside a shared frame.

That's operational alignment: not harmony, not consensus, not everyone liking the plan, but everyone knowing what "winning" looks like and what they're expected to trade off to get there.

If you're a producer, operational alignment is what makes planning real. If you're a lead, it's what makes execution consistent. Without it, you get local optimization: each discipline makes rational choices that are collectively irrational.

What "knowing what wins" actually means

When I say "everyone knows what wins," I mean four things are true at the same time:

First, the team can state the **current win condition** in plain language. Not a slogan. A practical definition of what success looks like for this phase of development.

Second, the team knows the **ranking of constraints**. When trade-offs appear – and they always will – people don't improvise based on personal preference. They follow the same priority order.

Third, people understand the **scope boundary**: what is in, what is out, and what is not allowed to quietly creep in.

Fourth, people can predict how decisions will be made, because ownership and decision rules are clear enough to avoid surprise reversals.

You'll notice none of this requires everyone to be happy. It requires clarity.

Operational alignment is the opposite of "we'll figure it out." It is "we already agreed what we're optimizing for, so we can move fast without asking permission for everything."

Why agreement is overrated and clarity is underrated

Producers often chase agreement because it reduces friction in the short term. Leads often chase agreement because it feels like unity. Both are understandable. Both are dangerous.

The reason agreement is overrated is simple: you can get agreement by making statements vague enough that nobody objects. That produces the worst outcome: everyone nods, everyone interprets it differently, everyone executes confidently, and then the build reveals you were never aligned.

Clarity creates friction early. It forces uncomfortable conversations about constraints, trade-offs, and cuts. But that friction is productive. It prevents expensive conflict later, when work is already done and emotions are higher.

If you remember only one thing: **alignment is not the absence of conflict; it's the presence of a shared decision frame.**

The four layers of operational alignment

To make this practical, think of operational alignment as four layers you keep consistent. When any layer is missing, teams start drifting.

Layer 1: Player value – what experience are we trying to win?

Games don't win by being "feature complete." They win by delivering a specific experience to a specific audience.

Operational alignment requires the team to know what experience is being optimized *right now*. Not in a fantasy future, but in the current build and the next milestone.

If your "direction" says "tense survival horror," the win condition in a given phase might be: "The first 30 minutes reliably produce tension without confusion." That tells design what to focus on, art what atmosphere must support, engineering what performance and readability constraints matter, and production what to protect from random scope additions.

Without this layer, teams can "improve" the game in ways that dilute it. Each improvement is rational locally, but it changes the identity of the product.

Layer 2: Business reality – what constraints are non-negotiable?

Games don't ship in a vacuum. You have runway, commitments, marketing beats, platform requirements, and sometimes publisher milestones. These constraints are not evil; they're physics.

Operational alignment means the team knows which business constraints are real and how they rank. Is the date hard and scope flexible? Is the scope fixed and date flexible? Is quality bar non-negotiable even if it means slip? Different projects can choose different answers. Chaos happens when the team pretends all constraints are non-negotiable at the same time.

The fastest way to break alignment is to hide business constraints until late. Then people feel betrayed: "Why are we cutting now?" The real answer is "because we never told you what was real."

Layer 3: Technical truth – what makes it shippable?

Engineering alignment isn't just about architecture. It's about what conditions must be true for the game to be reliably testable and deliverable.

If build stability is poor, nothing else matters. Your iteration loop is broken. If performance budgets are unknown, content will overrun them. If platform constraints are ignored, you'll pay later in painful rewrites.

Operational alignment requires the team to share the same "shippable definition," not just in QA terms but in system terms: stability, performance, save/load integrity, input responsiveness, memory, platform compliance.

This is also where leads often fight: creative wants more, tech wants stability. Alignment isn't about picking a winner. It's about deciding upfront what "wins" in this phase so both sides stop fighting the same battle every week.

Layer 4: Quality bar – what is "good enough," and where is it not negotiable?

Quality is not one thing. It's a set of bars that vary by feature and by phase.

Operational alignment means you define where the bar is high now, where it can be medium, and what can be deliberately rough without harming the product.

Chaos quality is accidental: some things get polished because someone cared, others stay broken because nobody owned them. Aligned quality is intentional: you choose where to spend perfection, and you accept imperfection elsewhere with eyes open.

This also prevents "we'll do it in polish" lies. If the bar is defined, "polish" becomes a real phase, not a magical rescue plan.

What operational alignment looks like in a normal week

If alignment is real, you can feel it in small behaviors:

A designer makes a call without asking permission because they know the win condition and constraints.

An artist pushes back on a request because it violates the current bar, and production supports the pushback.

An engineer says "no" to a risky change because build health is a priority this sprint, and everyone accepts it without drama.

A producer can say "we're cutting this" and it doesn't become a moral crisis, because the trade-offs were already agreed.

Notice what's missing: surprise.

The absence of surprise is one of the clearest signals of operational alignment. People may not like every decision, but they're rarely shocked by how decisions are made.

A practical way to phrase "what wins" without making a manifesto

Some narrative with examples, not a big bullet list, so here's a compact format that tends to work.

A good "what wins" statement sounds like:

"In this phase, we win if the build proves the core loop is compelling and readable for our target player, while staying inside stability and performance budgets, and protecting the milestone constraints we've committed to. If we need to trade off, we prioritize: player experience in the first hour, then stability/performance, then schedule commitments, and only then optional scope."

This is not a slogan. It's an operational contract.

You can keep it short. The value is not length. The value is that when pressure hits, your leads make the same trade-off decisions instead of fighting each other.

The producer/lead responsibility

Operational alignment doesn't happen because you "communicate more." It happens because you make winning legible.

Producers make it legible by forcing trade-offs into daylight and protecting the plan from fantasy constraints. Leads make it legible by translating direction into concrete decisions and enforcing the bar consistently.

If you do that, you don't need everyone to agree. You need everyone to know what wins – and to act like it.

That's operational alignment. And without it, every other tool you add will eventually become theater.

II. Pillars: how to phrase them, how many to have, how to test them with examples

Most teams either don't have pillars at all, or they have pillars that are useless.

Useless pillars sound inspiring, get printed on a slide, and then get ignored the first time the schedule gets tight. Useful pillars do the opposite: they reduce debate, speed up decisions, and make trade-offs predictable. They are not marketing. They are a decision tool.

In this series, pillars are allowed to be broader than "creative pillars." A game is not just experience; it's also shippability. If your pillars don't protect stability, performance, and scope discipline when needed, they won't protect anything.

The key idea: **a pillar is a rule for choosing, not a description of what you wish you were building.**

What a good pillar is (and isn't)

A good pillar is specific enough to guide action and narrow enough to exclude things. If it doesn't exclude anything, it's not a pillar. It's a compliment.

A pillar is also not a feature list. "Open world exploration" is a feature direction, not a pillar, unless you define what "exploration" means and what it must produce.

And a pillar is not a vague vibe word. "Immersive," "fun," "polished," "high quality" are not pillars. They don't create decisions. They create arguments.

When pillars work, they answer the question: "When two good ideas conflict, which one wins?"

How many pillars to have

The real number is smaller than most teams want.

If you have one pillar, it becomes dogma. If you have seven, nobody can remember them, and they become decoration.

In practice, the sweet spot is usually **three** for creative/experience, plus optionally **one operational guardrail** pillar when the project needs it. Not always, but often.

Why three? Because three is memorable, and it forces prioritization. It also mirrors how real trade-offs happen. Most decisions in games are not "good vs bad." They are "good vs good," and pillars are how you rank good.

If you need more than three to describe your game, you're probably describing features, not pillars.

If you feel nervous having only three, that's a good sign. It means you're actually choosing.

How to phrase pillars so they're usable

A pillar should be written as a testable statement. Not long. Not poetic. Something a lead can apply in a review without guessing what you meant.

A practical structure is:

Pillar = outcome + constraint (sometimes) + priority hint

Outcome: what the player must reliably feel/experience.

Constraint: what must be true for that outcome to count.

Priority hint: what this pillar beats when there's conflict.

Example of a bad pillar:

"Immersive combat."

It's vague and non-operational. Everyone will project their own meaning.

Example of a usable pillar:

"Combat must reward deliberate positioning and readable choices; if we add complexity, it must increase clarity, not cognitive load."

Now you can test it. You can cut things that add complexity without clarity. You can defend decisions consistently. Producers can price changes against it.

Another example, more operational:

"Stable and testable build is a feature: we do not trade build health for new content intake."

That's not a creative pillar, but it's an operational pillar that prevents entropy in the phases where build feedback loops matter most.

Notice what all usable pillars share: they contain a hidden "no." They implicitly forbid something.

That's why they work.

Good vs bad: common anti-patterns

Bad pillars usually fail in one of these ways.

They're too abstract: "Quality," "Innovation," "Fun."
They're actually features: "Crafting," "Open world," "Multiplayer."
They're contradictory: "Fast-paced tactical realism."
They're unowned: nobody can enforce them when pressure hits.
They're unranked: when pillars conflict, there is no rule for what wins.

A particularly common failure: pillars that describe the *dream* version of the game, not the *shippable* version. Teams then use pillars to justify endless scope because "it doesn't meet the pillar yet." That's not alignment. That's self-sabotage.

How to test pillars with examples (the only way that matters)

If you write pillars and you don't test them against decisions, they aren't pillars yet. They're draft text.

Testing pillars means taking real scenarios and asking: "Would these pillars produce a clear decision quickly?"

You can do this with three kinds of examples.

First: **a feature request**

Example: "Let's add a deeper crafting system."

Your pillars should make it clear whether crafting supports the core experience or dilutes it. If you can't decide quickly, your pillars are too vague.

Second: **a quality compromise**

Example: “We can hit the milestone if we ship with noticeable animation pop.”

Pillars should tell you whether readability and feel beat schedule, or whether schedule beats polish for this phase. Without that, every milestone becomes a fight.

Third: **a technical constraint**

Example: “This VFX approach tanks performance on target hardware.”

Pillars should tell you if performance is a guardrail. If it is, the decision is immediate: change the approach. If it isn’t, you accept the risk knowingly.

Testing is also where you find contradictions. If one pillar suggests “yes” and another suggests “no,” that’s not a failure. That’s reality. Pillars conflict. Your job is to rank them or refine wording so the conflict is resolvable.

A simple “pillar check” you can run in reviews

Example of a simple test that’s adaptable. Here it is. You can run it in a feature pitch, a design review, an art review, or a milestone scope discussion.

Ask three questions:

1. **Which pillar does this serve, specifically?**
   If the answer is “all of them,” it serves none. Make the link explicit.
2. **What does it cost us, and which pillar are we trading against?**
   This forces trade-offs into daylight. It prevents “small change” lies.
3. **If we ship without it, do we violate a pillar, or do we just feel uncomfortable?**
   This separates real identity risk from perfectionism and anxiety.

These questions work because they force specificity and ranking without requiring heavy process.

Making pillars production-grade: tie them to cuts, not just direction

Here's the uncomfortable truth: pillars that don't survive cutting are fake.

The moment you get schedule pressure, you will cut something. If pillars don't tell you what to cut first, they won't protect your game. They'll just become a guilt trip.

This is where producers and leads must cooperate.

Leads must be willing to say: "This does not serve a pillar; we cut it."

Producers must be willing to protect the pillars that define the game, not the backlog that defines the comfort zone.

The "broad pillars" approach helps here. A common pattern is to keep three creative pillars and one operational guardrail pillar that changes by phase.

In pre-production or early production, your operational pillar might be: "Fast learning beats completeness: we optimize for testable slices."

Near shipping, it might become: "Stability and compliance beat novelty: no new feature intake without explicit trade-offs."

Those are pillars too. They're pillars for winning the phase.

A final sanity check: can a new team member use your pillars?

If a new hire reads your pillars and still can't predict what will win in conflicts, your pillars are not operational yet.

Good pillars make decisions boring. That's the point. They remove drama from trade-offs. They make "no" defensible. They make "yes" consistent.

And in chaotic production, consistency is not a luxury. It's how you ship.

III. Constraints: technical, time, budget, platform, and content constraints

Most production chaos doesn't start with bad intentions. It starts with pretending constraints are optional.

A constraint is not a "limitation" you complain about. It's a boundary condition that defines what is possible. In a healthy project, constraints are visible, named, and treated as real. In an unhealthy one, constraints are discovered late, negotiated emotionally, or ignored until they explode into schedule slips and crunch.

In this chapter we're talking about constraints as alignment tools. Not as a checklist you file away, but as the physics of the project. Producers and leads need to share a "constraint stack": multiple hard realities that must hold at the same time, plus a clear understanding of which ones are brittle and which ones can flex.

Let's frame this as risk. Constraints are risks when they're unclear, unmeasured, or unenforced.

Why constraints matter for operational alignment

Alignment is not "we all want the same thing." Alignment is "we all make the same trade-offs under pressure."

Constraints are what pressure pushes against. If you don't define them, you don't get trade-offs – you get denial.

Most teams fail here in one of two ways.

One: they define constraints too late. They build an imaginary version of the game, then get forced into painful cuts when reality arrives.

Two: they define constraints vaguely. "We should hit 60 FPS," "we need to ship this year," "we can't exceed budget." Those statements don't change behavior unless they turn into specific limits with owners and checkpoints.

A constraint only helps when it can say "no" in time.

Technical constraints: the ones you can't "motivate" away

Technical constraints are often treated like engineering preferences. That's a mistake. In games, technical constraints define whether the product is even testable, stable, and shippable.

The core technical constraints most projects carry include build stability, performance budgets, memory budgets, loading/streaming, save integrity, tooling limits, and engine/platform quirks. You don't need all of them on day one, but you need to know which ones are "silent killers" for your particular game.

Here's the key risk mechanism: technical constraints tend to be nonlinear. You can ignore them for months and feel fine, then suddenly you hit a wall and the project becomes a constant firefight. Performance and memory are classic examples: early content is light, everything runs. Later, content density increases and you discover the real cost of your systems. Fixing it late is expensive because you have more content built on top of the wrong assumptions.

Build stability is similar. If the build is fragile, your feedback loop is slow. Slow feedback makes decisions weaker. Weak decisions create thrash. Thrash creates more instability. Technical constraints can start a full entropy loop by themselves.

A practical lead mindset: treat build health as a product feature. If players can't play, you can't learn. If you can't learn, you can't align.

Time constraints: dates are only real if they force trade-offs

Time constraints are the most abused constraint category, because teams love dates and hate the trade-offs that make dates real.

A time constraint is not "we want to ship in Q4." A time constraint is "we are willing to cut scope to hit Q4, and we will actually do it."

The risk is obvious: when time is treated as fixed and scope is treated as fixed, the only remaining variable is people. That's how crunch becomes the hidden tool.

Time constraints also interact with learning. Early phases need faster learning cycles; late phases need stability. If you don't align on what the time constraint means for the current phase, you get the worst mismatch: late-phase expectations with early-phase uncertainty, or early-phase freedom with late-phase commitments.

A producer's job is not to "protect the schedule." It's to make time constraints honest: if a date is real, something else becomes flexible, and everyone knows what that is.

Budget constraints: runway is the ultimate truth teller

Budget constraints in most studios are not line-item accounting. They're runway: how many months you can fund the project before you must ship, secure funding, or shut down.

Runway constraints matter because they are unforgiving and usually invisible to the wider team. Leads may be making quality decisions as if the project has time to mature, while production is quietly watching the runway collapse. That gap breeds mistrust and late, brutal cuts.

There's also a second-order effect: runway pressure distorts decision-making. It encourages "short-term visible progress" over "long-term foundations." That's how you get a project that looks productive while becoming increasingly unshippable.

To keep budget constraints from turning into panic, you need two things: clarity and cadence. Clarity means the team knows which milestones are tied to funding or commercial commitments. Cadence means you review burn-to-output regularly enough that you can adjust early rather than crash late.

This isn't about sharing sensitive numbers with everyone. It's about ensuring the people making scope and quality decisions understand the boundary conditions.

Platform constraints: small on paper, brutal in reality

Let's go light on console certification specifics, so I'll keep this at the right altitude.

Platform constraints are dangerous because they tend to arrive as "requirements" that look minor until you implement them. Input standards, UI safe zones, save behavior, performance targets, loading rules, compliance requirements, and platform-specific edge cases can all reshape systems late.

Even outside consoles, platform constraints show up as hardware variability, storefront rules, patch workflows, controller support expectations, localization requirements, accessibility expectations, and community standards.

The risk pattern is consistent: platform constraints are ignored early because they "don't affect the core fun." Then they affect the core fun because they force rework in systems you assumed were done.

The anti-chaos move is simple: treat platform constraints as part of definition of done for key systems early enough that they don't become endgame surprises.

Content constraints: the silent scope killer

Content constraints are where many teams truly die, because content is addictive. You can always add more. And adding content feels like progress, even when it destroys focus.

Content constraints include asset volume, production throughput, iteration bandwidth, pipeline friction, review capacity, VO/localization cost, level count, quest density, narrative branching, and the "integration tax" of every new piece.

The special risk with content constraints is that they multiply technical and QA load. Every new asset increases memory and performance pressure. Every new quest increases test cases. Every new line of VO increases localization complexity. Every new level increases bug surface area. If you don't cap content intake, you can keep "producing" while secretly making shipping harder.

A common anti-pattern is content production running ahead of design stability. Artists and narrative teams produce lots of material to "stay busy," while the game's direction is still shifting. Later you cut or redo large chunks. That's not because content teams failed. It's because the project had no content constraints and no clear "what wins" boundary.

Content constraints are not anti-creative. They protect creativity by preventing you from drowning in your own output.

The constraint stack: how these interact

In real production you don't have one constraint. You have a stack.

Time pushes you toward cutting.
Budget pushes you toward certainty and de-risking.
Technical pushes you toward stability and early integration.
Platform pushes you toward compliance and predictable behavior.
Content pushes you toward caps and throughput realism.

Chaos happens when different roles optimize for different constraints without a shared ranking. A lead might optimize for quality and direction. A producer might optimize for time and runway. Engineering might optimize for stability. Everyone is "right," but the system becomes a tug-of-war.

Operational alignment means you agree on the stack and how to resolve conflicts, before the conflict hits.

A simple "constraint contract" example

This is intentionally short. You can paste something like this into a project doc, milestone page, or even a pinned message. The goal is not formality. The goal is enforceability.

Constraint Contract (Phase: Next 6 Weeks)

We are optimizing for a playable, stable slice that validates the core loop and the first-hour experience.

Hard constraints (must hold):

Build must remain reliably testable; we do not accept prolonged instability as "normal."
Performance must stay within agreed targets for the primary platform; no new content intake that breaks budgets without explicit trade-off.

Runway dictates we hit the milestone; if we slip, we cut scope, not sleep.

Soft constraints (can flex with explicit decision):

Secondary features can be reduced or simplified.
Non-critical content volume can be capped or postponed.
Visual polish outside the first-hour experience can be deferred.

Measurement / checkpoints:

Weekly build health check with leads; if instability trends up, feature intake pauses until stabilized.

Bi-weekly content intake review; if QA surface is expanding faster than capacity, content scope is capped.

Milestone scope review every two weeks; any new priority must name what it replaces.

Owners:
Build stability owner: Tech lead.
Content intake owner: Producer + content lead.
Milestone scope owner: Producer (with direction owner consulted).
Platform compliance awareness: Relevant lead per platform target.

This kind of contract works because it turns constraints into shared reality with visible enforcement. It also avoids the trap of pretending everything is equally important.

A final sanity check for producers and leads

If your constraints don't change behavior, they're not constraints. They're opinions.

A good constraint stack produces predictable "no's" early, so you don't pay for chaotic "no's" late. And that's what operational alignment is really buying you: fewer surprises, fewer reversals, less rework, and a project that can actually ship under its real physics.

IV. Nongoals: explicit "what we will NOT do" as a weapon against scope creep

Most teams try to fight scope creep with discipline, motivation, and better planning. That's fine, but it's weak armor.

The strongest anti-scope tool is simpler and more brutal: **explicit nongoals.**

A nongoal is not a "nice-to-have we probably won't get to." It's a declared boundary: what you will *not* do, even if it's a good idea, even if someone senior wants it, even if it would be "cool," unless you pay for it by removing something else.

Nongoals don't reduce creativity. They reduce decision noise. They turn a constant stream of seductive ideas into a controlled trade-off process.

If you work with publisher milestones, nongoals become even more valuable. Publishers don't just buy your vision. They buy your predictability. Nongoals are how you keep the project predictable without becoming rigid.

Where nongoals should live (so they actually work)

Put them in one place that is impossible to ignore, and that is close to decision-making. The best home is your **milestone one-pager** (or milestone brief): a short document that everyone references when questions come up.

Why there? Because scope creep rarely arrives as "let's expand scope." It arrives as a "reasonable request" in the context of a milestone: "Can we also…?" "We should add…?" "It would be better if…?" If nongoals live next to the milestone goals, they have a chance to block that request before it turns into work.

Second-best is a pinned message in your main project channel that links to the one-pager. Backlog is a weak home because it's too easy to hide scope creep inside tasks. Wiki is a weak home because people don't visit it under pressure. The point of nongoals is fast friction at the moment of temptation.

Why nongoals work when "priorities" don't

"Priorities" are positive statements. They tell you what you want to do. They don't tell you what you will refuse.

Scope creep feeds on ambiguity. If you don't explicitly refuse things, everything becomes negotiable. People interpret silence as permission. They assume "maybe later" means "eventually," and eventually becomes now.

Nongoals are negative clarity. They're uncomfortable, which is exactly why they're effective. They force the team to confront trade-offs early, while the cost is still manageable.

They also protect leads. Without nongoals, a lead who says "no" looks stubborn. With nongoals, the lead is enforcing an agreed boundary. That changes the social dynamics: "no" stops being personal and becomes operational.

What good nongoals look like

A good nongoal is specific enough that you can apply it in a meeting without debate. If it's too vague, it becomes a loophole.

Bad nongoal: "No scope creep."

That's just a wish.

Better nongoal: "No new core systems after milestone lock."

Even better: "No new core systems after vertical slice approval without cutting an existing system of similar size."

You also want nongoals to cover the most common creep vectors. In mixed teams, the usual suspects are content volume, "small changes," quality inflation, platform expansion, and tool ambitions.

Examples that tend to be useful across projects:

You are not adding new platforms in this phase.
You are not expanding content volume beyond the agreed cap (levels, quests, weapons, enemies, VO lines).
You are not introducing new mechanics that require tutorialization.
You are not rewriting major systems unless they block the core loop.
You are not promising features to the community that aren't already committed internally.

You are not accepting late "drive-by improvements" without removing something else.

You can include technical nongoals too, carefully. A classic one is "no tool-building projects disguised as 'quick fixes'." Tooling matters, but uncontrolled tooling is one of the fastest ways to lose months.

The point is not to cover everything. The point is to block the patterns that have historically killed projects.

How many nongoals to have, and how they can change by phase

Keep them short. If you have ten, nobody remembers them and you'll end up selectively enforcing them. That destroys trust.

In practice, **five** is a good number for a milestone phase. Enough to cover major creep vectors, small enough to be memorable.

And yes: they can be phase-dependent.

Early phases often have nongoals that protect learning. For example: "We won't add content volume; we'll validate the loop."

Mid production often has nongoals that protect throughput. For example: "We won't add new systems that expand QA surface."

Late production has nongoals that protect stability. For example: "We won't introduce new feature intake; we only fix, tune, and stabilize."

This is how you stay adaptive without becoming chaotic: you change boundaries deliberately, not accidentally.

The hard part: exceptions and trade-offs without turning nongoals into jokes

The fastest way to kill nongoals is to break them casually. The second fastest is to treat them as absolute and then secretly violate them anyway.

The right approach is an explicit exception rule that forces a real trade.

Here's the principle: **a nongoal can be broken only if you pay for it immediately with a comparable cut, and the owner signs it.**

Comparable means comparable in risk and load, not just in "task count." If you add a system that expands QA surface and tutorial needs, you cut something that also expands QA surface and tutorial needs. Cutting two cosmetics doesn't pay for a new mechanic.

You don't need a committee. You need ownership and a short ritual.

A practical exception flow looks like this:

Someone proposes breaking a nongoal.
They must name the reason in one sentence and what new evidence changed.
They must propose a cut of comparable cost and risk.
The relevant owners approve: usually producer + direction owner + impacted lead (often tech for build/architecture, or content lead for content intake).
The decision is recorded and communicated as a trade, not as "additional work."

This does two things. It makes exceptions rare, because they now require pain. And when exceptions happen, they don't destabilize the system, because the trade-off is explicit.

How to phrase the "trade-off" so people accept it

This is where producers and leads either build trust or lose it.

If you say "we can't do that," people feel shut down.

If you say "we can do it if we cut something else," you're treating them like adults and protecting the project.

The language matters. A calm, direct phrasing that works:

"We can break this nongoal, but only as an explicit trade. What do we remove to pay for it, and are we willing to accept that consequence?"

This shifts the conversation from taste to constraints, from politics to decisions. It also educates the team over time: ideas aren't rejected because they're bad, they're rejected because they don't fit the win conditions of this phase.

Nongoals as an anti-scope culture tool

Over time, nongoals create a healthier culture because they remove guilt and ambiguity.

People stop sneaking scope in "because it's small."

They stop using polish as a magical rescue phase.

They stop waiting for the latest opinion and start executing against a stable frame.

And with publishers, there's another benefit: nongoals make milestone conversations more professional. Instead of defending delays with excuses, you can show a controlled decision system: "We protected the milestone by refusing these expansions; when we made an exception, we paid for it explicitly."

That's credibility. And credibility buys you flexibility later.

If you want to fight scope creep effectively, don't just say what you're doing. Say what you will not do. Then enforce it with real trade-offs, not with hope.

V. The minimum document: a project one-pager (what must be there, what is noise)

If you want operational alignment in pre-production, you need one document that actually gets used. Not a pitch deck. Not a lore bible. Not a 40-page “vision doc” nobody updates. A one-pager.

A project one-pager is not about capturing everything you know. It’s about preventing the team from building three different versions of the same game in their heads.

In pre-prod, your biggest risk is not “we don’t have enough details.” Your biggest risk is “we have too many interpretations.” The one-pager exists to collapse interpretation space early, so your iteration has a stable frame.

This is why I call it the minimum document. Everything else is optional until the one-pager is good.

What a one-pager is for (and what it is not)

A one-pager is a decision reference. It answers “what wins” and “what we are not doing” in a way the whole team can repeat.

It is not a marketing doc. It is not a design spec. It is not a replacement for a backlog. If you treat it like any of those, it becomes noise.

A good one-pager has one job: **when someone asks “should we do X?” the one-pager helps you decide quickly.**

Should it be a living doc or a milestone brief?

In pre-production, make it a **living doc with a strict update rhythm**, otherwise it becomes stale and people stop trusting it.

The trick is to update it lightly but consistently. Not “rewrite the doc weekly.” Just keep it current in the few sections that matter: pillars, constraints, nongoals, and the next validation goal. If you update those, the one-pager stays credible.

A practical cadence that works: a short review in a weekly lead sync, with the producer owning the edit. If nothing changed, that's a decision too. You still confirm: "this is still the frame."

Later, when you enter production and milestones become fixed, the same doc can evolve into a milestone brief. But in pre-prod, it's a living alignment tool.

What must be on the one-pager (minimum viable alignment)

You said the primary reader is the whole team, so the content has to be readable and non-theoretical. Every section must help someone decide or execute.

The minimum set looks like this:

First, a one-sentence **game direction statement**. Not a slogan. A practical description of the intended experience, target player, and the "promise" of the game. If the sentence can describe ten different games, it's too vague.

Second, **three pillars** that actually exclude things. Pillars are the rules for choosing. If someone can't use them in a review, they're decoration.

Third, **win conditions for the current phase**. In pre-prod, this is usually what you're trying to validate next (core loop viability, first-hour clarity, combat feel, etc.). This keeps the team from "building everything a bit."

Fourth, a **constraint stack** that makes trade-offs real. Time, budget/runway reality, tech constraints (build health/performance budgets), platform assumptions, and content constraints. These don't have to be precise yet, but they must be explicit.

Fifth, **nongoals.** This is where scope creep dies. If you don't say "we will NOT do X," you will quietly do X.

Sixth, **definition of done for the phase**. Not production-grade "done" yet, but what "done enough to learn" means. This prevents people from polishing prematurely or shipping untestable slices.

Seventh, **ownership and decision paths**. Not org charts. Just who owns direction, who owns build health, who owns content intake, and how decisions become real (your mini decision contract logic). If people don't know who decides, they will decide implicitly, and you're back to shadow decisions.

That's it. Everything else is optional until these are solid.

What is noise (and why it's tempting)

In pre-production, noise is anything that feels productive but doesn't help decisions.

Common noise sources you should actively resist:

Lore dumps and world-building that isn't used to validate the core experience. It might be fun, but it doesn't align production unless your game is literally narrative-first and you're testing narrative delivery.

Feature lists without trade-offs. Lists create scope creep because they read like promises. They also create fake progress: "we planned it, so it's real."

"Detailed" design specs for systems that haven't been proven. Pre-prod is for validation, not for writing future regret.

Roadmaps built on hope. A roadmap that assumes every idea survives contact with iteration is not a plan. It's wishful thinking.

Pseudo-metrics. "We'll have X hours of gameplay," "Y weapons," "Z enemies" before you even know what the loop needs. In pre-prod, these numbers are usually lies you'll later defend emotionally.

Complex diagrams and elaborate processes. If your one-pager requires training to understand, it will not be used. The one-pager is meant to reduce cognitive load, not add it.

The rule is simple: if a section doesn't change behavior next week, it's noise.

Making it "publisher milestone ready" without turning it into a pitch deck

Even if the one-pager is internal, you should write it in a way that can be shared externally with minimal edits. That's a useful forcing function. It keeps you honest.

You don't need publisher formatting. You need publisher clarity: what you're building, what you're validating next, what constraints are real, and what you're not promising.

A small "external-ready" addition that's worth having is a short line on deliverable intent for the next checkpoint, plus **acceptance criteria** phrased as observable outcomes. Not a big contract. Just enough that you can align internally and avoid "we thought this milestone meant X."

This also protects you if you do have a publisher: the internal team doesn't drift into a different interpretation of the milestone than the external stakeholder.

A practical template you can copy

Below is a one-page template that is deliberately tight. You can paste it into a doc, wiki page, or a pinned message. Keep it to one page. If you need more, you probably need better phrasing, not more content.

PROJECT ONE-PAGER (Pre-Production)
Project name: [Working Title]
Version / date: [v0.3 – YYYY-MM-DD]
Owner: [Producer name]

1) Direction (one sentence)
We are making a [genre] game for [target player] where the core promise is [core experience], and we win when [primary feeling/outcome] happens reliably.

2) Pillars (3 rules for choosing)
P1: [Outcome + constraint – what must always be true]
P2: [Outcome + constraint – what we optimize for]
P3: [Outcome + constraint – what we refuse to dilute]

3) Current phase win condition (what "wins" in the next X weeks)
We win this phase if we can validate:

- [Core loop validation outcome]
- [First-hour/UX/readability outcome]
- [Technical feasibility outcome: build stability/performance budget]
  If we must trade off, priority order is: [Player value] > [Stability/Performance] > [Milestone/date reality] > [Optional scope].

4) Constraint stack (what is real physics right now)
Time: [Next checkpoint date / window]
Budget/runway: [High-level reality: months / milestone dependency]
Technical: [Build health expectations + performance/memory assumptions]
Platform: [Primary target platform(s) + any hard assumptions]
Content: [Caps or boundaries: "we are not scaling content volume yet"]

5) Nongoals (what we will NOT do in this phase)
We will NOT:

- [Example: add new core systems beyond the loop under test]
- [Example: expand to additional platforms]
- [Example: build large content volume before loop is proven]
- [Example: promise features externally not validated internally]
  Exceptions require an explicit trade

6) Definition of done (for pre-prod deliverables)
A deliverable is "done" when: it is playable, testable, and produces feedback against the phase win condition.
"Done" does NOT mean fully polished. "Done" means we can learn.

7) Decision rules (how trade-offs happen)
Any change that affects scope, pillars, constraints, or nongoals must be recorded as a decision: Decision / Owner / Why / Trade-off / Impact / Commit signal / Revisit rule.
Breaking a nongoal requires: proposed cut of comparable risk + approval by [Producer + Direction Owner + impacted lead].

8) Owners (who keeps what coherent)
Direction owner: [Name/role]
Build health owner: [Name/role]
Content intake owner: [Name/role]
Milestone scope owner: [Name/role]

How to keep the one-pager clean over time

The document will naturally bloat because people will try to use it as a dumping ground. Don't allow that.

When someone wants to add a section, ask: "Which decision will this change next week?" If there isn't one, it doesn't belong on the one-pager. Put it elsewhere or don't write it yet.

Also, treat every update as a decision. If you change a pillar, that's not "editing text." That's changing what wins. That needs visibility and trade-offs.

The payoff

A good one-pager does something rare in gamedev: it makes execution predictable without killing creativity.

It allows turbulence inside a frame. It gives producers and leads a shared language for trade-offs. And it gives the whole team one source of truth that's light enough to stay alive.

If you can keep this one page sharp, most of your alignment work becomes easier. If you can't, everything else you write will be noise.

VI. How to validate alignment: typical conflicts (UX vs perf, art vs runtime, fun vs cert)

Alignment is easy when there is no pressure. Everyone agrees in the abstract. The real test is conflict.

If your project claims to be aligned, you should be able to predict how it resolves the same conflicts again and again. If every conflict turns into a fresh debate from scratch, you don't have operational alignment. You have temporary cooperation.

Validation is not a survey. It's not "does everyone feel aligned?" Validation is observing decision behavior under stress and checking whether it matches your declared pillars, constraints, and "what wins" frame.

This section gives you a practical method to validate alignment using the conflicts that reliably expose it: UX vs performance, art vs runtime constraints, and fun vs certification/platform rules.

The basic method: do we resolve conflicts with a shared frame or with politics?

When a conflict appears, there are only two ways teams resolve it:

They use a shared decision frame: pillars + constraint stack + current phase win condition, ideally captured in the one-pager. The outcome may still be painful, but it is predictable and explainable.

Or they resolve it through politics and fatigue: the loudest voice, the most senior person, the person who can block the build, or the last person who spoke in the meeting. That creates resentment and randomness, which is how alignment collapses.

So the validation question is simple: **when conflict hits, do we reference "what wins," or do we improvise?**

If you want this to work in real life, you need to treat conflicts as tests you can pass or fail. You don't "hope" alignment exists. You prove it by the way you decide.

Conflict 1: UX vs performance

This one shows up everywhere and in every phase.

The UX side wants clarity, responsiveness, and a smoother player experience: richer UI, more feedback, heavier effects, more tutorial support, more reactive systems.

The performance side wants stable framerate, predictable input latency, memory budgets, and no spikes. Especially on constrained hardware or when content density increases late.

The conflict is not "UX vs perf." It's "what do we prioritize when we cannot have both at once?"

How you validate alignment here is by watching what happens when someone proposes a UX improvement that threatens performance, or when engineering proposes performance optimizations that harm readability or feel.

Aligned behavior looks like this: you run a pillar check and a constraint check. You ask: does the UX change improve a pillar outcome, or is it cosmetic? Is performance currently a hard constraint for this phase? What is the win condition for the next milestone: player experience in the first hour, or stability and compliance?

If your current frame says "first-hour clarity wins," you might accept a controlled performance cost temporarily, but only with explicit limits and a plan to measure and recover. If your frame says "stability/perf is a guardrail this phase," the UX change must be redesigned until it fits within budgets.

Misaligned behavior looks like this: UX pushes until engineering reluctantly agrees, then later engineering "takes it back" under pressure, or engineering refuses without offering alternatives, and UX interprets it as sabotage. In both cases, the decision feels personal because the frame is missing.

A simple validation signal: do UX vs perf conflicts end with a clear rule that can be repeated next week? Or do they end with a one-off compromise nobody can explain?

If it's one-off, alignment is weak.

Conflict 2: Art vs runtime constraints

This is one of the most dangerous conflicts because it is emotionally loaded. Art is visible. Runtime constraints are invisible until they ruin the build.

The typical pattern is predictable. Art pushes for fidelity, variety, density, and "wow." Runtime pushes back with frame budget, memory budget, streaming, draw calls, shader complexity, and platform variance. If the project is misaligned, the conversation turns into "art doesn't care about performance" vs "engineering kills beauty." That is not a technical problem. It's an alignment problem.

Validation here is about whether your project has operational pillars and constraints that connect art choices to runtime reality early.

Aligned behavior looks like this: art and engineering share an explicit performance and memory budget target, plus content constraints, plus a definition of done that includes "runs within budget on target hardware." The conflict resolution is not "lower quality." It's "choose where quality matters most," using pillars.

For example, if one pillar is "readability under stress," you might choose fewer materials and cleaner silhouettes rather than higher poly counts everywhere. If a pillar is "atmosphere through lighting," you invest budget there and simplify elsewhere.

Misaligned behavior looks like this: you discover runtime constraints late, after content has been built beyond budgets. Then you "optimize" by cutting corners everywhere: reducing quality uniformly, sacrificing coherence, creating more rework, and demoralizing teams. That's entropy.

A strong validation test: can the team answer, without drama, "what do we optimize visually, and what do we deliberately simplify?" If not, you don't have alignment. You have taste disagreements waiting to explode.

Another validation test: does the project have an early "budget truth moment" where art content is tested on target constraints, not just on a dev machine? If not, you're not validating; you're postponing.

Conflict 3: Fun vs certification / platform rules

This one is often dismissed until late, then becomes a crisis.

"Certification" here is shorthand for platform rules, compliance expectations, and ecosystem constraints. Even outside consoles, you have rules: save behavior, suspend/resume expectations, input requirements, error handling, network behavior, content guidelines, storefront policies. These constraints can collide with what feels "fun," "smooth," or "immersive."

Misaligned teams treat this as an external annoyance. They keep building the "fun" version and plan to "handle cert later." Then late-stage compliance work forces awkward changes in UX and flow, which triggers conflict and rework when time is tight.

Aligned teams treat platform rules as part of the constraint stack and embed them into definition of done early for the systems that interact with them: saving, loading, pausing, input, stability, error states.

Validation here is about whether your project can say: "fun is the goal, but we do not ship a fun experience that violates platform reality, because that isn't shippable fun."

This is where operational alignment becomes real: can the team accept that a great feature is not a great feature if it cannot ship?

A practical validation signal: when someone says "this would be fun," does anyone ask, calmly, "is it shippable under our platform constraints?" If that question never appears, you're not aligned on the constraint stack.

How to validate alignment systematically, not emotionally

The mistake teams make is treating conflicts as interpersonal events. They are system events. Here's a simple validation flow you can run whenever a conflict appears, without turning it into ceremony.

First, identify what kind of conflict it is: pillar vs pillar, pillar vs constraint, or constraint vs constraint.

Then, anchor the discussion to the shared frame:

- Which pillar does each side claim to serve?
- Which constraint does each side claim to protect?

- What is the current phase win condition?

If you can't answer those questions quickly, you've found the problem. Your one-pager is either missing content, too vague, or not trusted.

Next, force trade-offs into daylight. Every conflict resolution must name what loses. If nobody can say what loses, the decision is fake.

Finally, make the decision repeatable: capture one sentence that becomes the default rule until new evidence appears. That is the actual output of alignment.

The biggest red flags that alignment is not real

For analysis and validation; here are the signals that your "alignment" is performative.

The same conflict repeats weekly with no convergence.

Decisions reverse late because someone with authority was not part of the frame.
Trade-offs are avoided; scope and quality are treated as simultaneously fixed.
Build feedback is too weak to provide truth, so debates are based on opinion.
People argue about process and fairness more than about the product.
"Small changes" are accepted without blast-radius checks, then performance and cert explode later.

If you see these, stop asking "are we aligned?" and start asking "which part of our frame is missing?"

Because real alignment is not a feeling. It's a behavior pattern you can validate under conflict.

VII. Keeping alignment over time: "re-alignment" rituals (when, with whom, in what format)

Alignment is not something you "achieve." It's something you maintain.

Every game project drifts. New information appears, constraints change, people get tired, stakeholders show up, the build reveals uncomfortable truths. If you don't have a way to re-align, your one-pager becomes propaganda: it describes what you *wish* was true, while the project quietly becomes something else.

The goal of re-alignment rituals is not to add meetings. It's to create a predictable moment where the project updates its shared frame: what wins, what doesn't, what changed, and what we're doing about it.

And yes, alignment must work in both directions. The one-pager is not leadership's weapon to force compliance. It's the team's tool to keep reality and intent synced. If reality changed, the document must change. If the document doesn't match reality, either the project is lying to itself or the team is being punished for learning.

The core idea: drift is normal, unacknowledged drift is lethal

You should assume drift will happen. The question is whether drift is surfaced early, translated into decisions, and absorbed into the operating system of the project.

Re-alignment is how you avoid two failure modes that look opposite but are equally deadly:

One: **direction fantasy** – the doc stays idealistic while the build and backlog diverge. People keep saying the words, but they don't mean them anymore.

Two: **direction panic** – the doc changes every week based on mood, feedback, or fear, and the team loses trust in any stable frame.

Healthy re-alignment sits between those: reality updates the frame, but the frame stays stable enough to execute.

A "healthy set" of rituals, without ceremony bloat

Teams vary, so instead of prescribing one calendar, think of re-alignment as three layers. You can adopt all three, or start with one and grow as needed.

Layer one is a **micro re-alignment** that happens frequently and cheaply. It's lead-level, short, and focused on drift signals.

Layer two is a **regular cadence re-alignment** (often per sprint or bi-weekly) that confirms the frame and updates the one-pager if required.

Layer three is an **event-driven re-alignment** triggered by major changes: milestones, pivots, big constraints, publisher moments, major playtest results, build health collapses, platform expansion, budget/runway shifts.

This structure works because it doesn't force heavy meetings when nothing is changing, but it guarantees you don't ignore drift when reality moves.

When to re-align: set triggers, not just dates

If you want the team to choose a standard, don't ask them "how often do you want alignment?" Ask them two questions:

What is the maximum drift you can tolerate before decisions become expensive?
What signals reliably tell you drift is happening?

Then set a cadence that catches drift before the cost spikes.

The most common healthy triggers are boring and practical:

A significant change in scope or priorities.
A shift in constraints (time, budget/runway, platform, performance targets).
A meaningful playtest/market feedback event that invalidates assumptions.
A build stability drop that breaks the feedback loop.
A milestone handoff (internal or publisher-facing).
A change in key decision owners (lead changes, leadership reorg, new stakeholder).

A repeated conflict pattern that keeps resurfacing (UX vs perf, art vs runtime, fun vs compliance) with no convergence.

The reason to formalize triggers is simple: if you rely only on "we'll re-align when it feels needed," you will re-align too late, because people avoid friction when they're busy.

With whom: don't invite everyone to everything

Alignment is not a democracy, but it also cannot be a private leadership club. The right audience depends on the type of drift you're addressing.

Most of the time, the most effective default is **producer + core leads** (design, tech, art; plus QA or release owner if relevant). That's where trade-offs can actually be made and enforced.

Then you decide what needs to be propagated to the wider team. If re-alignment changes pillars, nongoals, constraints, or the phase win condition, the whole team must see it quickly. Not as a 90-minute meeting. As a short, explicit update tied to the one-pager.

A useful rule: decision-making is small, decision visibility is large. Keep the decision room tight, but make the results impossible to miss.

Also, occasionally you need "two-way" input, not just broadcast. If the team is experiencing recurring rework, constant re-prioritization, or build pain, that's not "execution failure." That's your frame failing to match reality. You need signals from the people doing the work. Otherwise the one-pager becomes a lie.

In what format: the three practical re-alignment formats

Here are the three formats that cover almost everything, without turning your studio into a meeting factory.

Format A: the 15-minute lead check-in (micro re-alignment)

Use this weekly or whenever the project feels "off."

The purpose is not to solve big issues. The purpose is to catch drift early and decide whether you need a deeper re-alignment.

A micro check-in works when it answers three questions quickly:
Are we still optimizing for the same "win" this week?
Did any constraint become tighter since last week?
Did we make any decision that contradicts our pillars/nongoals?

If you can't answer those quickly, you don't need a longer meeting yet. You need a clearer frame.

The output of this format is usually one of two things: "no change" or "we need a re-alignment session on X."

Format B: the 30–60 minute re-alignment session (regular cadence)

Use this per sprint, bi-weekly, or monthly depending on volatility. Teams in heavy iteration need it more often; teams in stable production can do it less frequently.

This is where you actually update the one-pager. The session is successful if it produces explicit changes or explicit confirmation.

A healthy structure is: reality first, then frame, then decisions.

Reality: what changed in the build, in constraints, in stakeholder needs, in learning?
Frame: do pillars/constraints/nongoals still match reality and the intended direction?
Decisions: what do we change, what do we cut, what do we freeze, what becomes the next validation goal?

The key is discipline: the one-pager is not "notes from the meeting." It is the result. If you leave the meeting and the one-pager doesn't change while reality did, you did theater.

Format C: the 60–120 minute event-driven alignment reset (when reality punches you)

This is for major moments: milestone failure, significant pivot, platform expansion, severe build health issues, publisher escalation, major playtest invalidation, runway shock.
This format is not about re-litigating everything. It's about choosing the minimum set of frame changes that restore predictability.

The danger in these moments is either denial ("we can still do everything") or overreaction ("rewrite the whole plan"). A good reset picks a few critical constraints and makes them real immediately.

In this format, you explicitly decide: what is now hard, what is now soft, what gets cut, and what the next "win condition" is that proves the project is back under control.

Re-alignment that works in both directions

You said it clearly: the one-pager, pillars, nongoals, and constraints exist for a reason. If they don't update based on what the team learns, they're useless.

Two-way alignment means you treat execution signals as input to the frame. Not just output from the frame.

If the team repeatedly can't hit the planned scope without heroics, that's not "lack of discipline." That's a constraint mismatch.

If art repeatedly can't meet runtime budgets, that's not "art being unrealistic." That's a budget definition or pipeline mismatch.

If UX keeps losing to perf in ad hoc fights, that's not "engineering being stubborn." That's missing priorities in the constraint stack.

The one-pager should be updated from these signals. Otherwise you're not aligning; you're commanding.

A practical habit: whenever you see repeated conflict or repeated rework, treat it as a trigger to ask "what in our alignment frame is unclear or false?" That question alone prevents a lot of blame cycles.

How to help a team choose the right standard cadence

Teams should choose cadence based on volatility, not on preference.

If your project is in heavy learning mode (pre-prod, vertical slice, major gameplay iteration), you need more frequent micro checks and at least a bi-weekly frame update. Drift happens fast because learning happens fast.

If your project is in stable production (content throughput, predictable pipeline, known constraints), weekly micro checks might be enough and the deeper re-alignment can be monthly or milestone-based.

If your project is late-stage (stability, compliance, shipping), re-alignment should be driven by triggers: build health, cert risks, critical bugs, scope changes. In late stage, the cost of frame changes is high, so you don't want to churn the frame. You want to protect it.

The simplest rule to communicate: the more unknowns you're actively reducing, the more often you re-align. The more you are executing known work, the less often you re-align – unless reality changes.

What "good" looks like over time

You'll know re-alignment is working when two things become true:

Conflicts resolve faster because people reference the same frame, not because they avoid conflict.

The one-pager stays short, current, and trusted because it matches reality and decisions.

If instead you see the one-pager growing, drifting, or being ignored, your rituals are either too heavy (people avoid them) or too weak (they don't change anything).

Re-alignment is not about meetings. It's about keeping your shared operating system honest.

If you do that consistently, alignment stops being a fragile feeling and becomes a durable habit – one that survives iteration, pressure, and inevitable surprises.

VIII. Anti-pattern: a "vision deck" with no decisions and no impact on the backlog

A vision deck is not automatically bad. It becomes an anti-pattern when it turns into a substitute for decisions.

You've seen this: a beautiful slide deck. Strong statements. References. Moodboards. A "direction" that sounds confident. People nod. Maybe the publisher is impressed. Maybe the team feels inspired for a day.

Then Monday comes. The backlog looks the same. Priorities are unchanged. Trade-offs are still unresolved. Decisions are still soft. The deck becomes a poster on the wall while the project runs on improvisation.

That's the anti-pattern: **a vision deck that produces no decisions and has no measurable impact on what the team actually builds.**

The guiding example: "Project Atlas" and the deck that changed nothing

Let's use one realistic scenario.

Project Atlas is in pre-production. The creative lead and CEO want a strong direction, especially because they're talking to a publisher. They assemble a vision deck: tone, pillars, references, "player fantasy," key features. It's well-made. It feels serious.

In the review meeting, everyone agrees it's "the right direction." Nobody wants to be the person who ruins the mood by talking about constraints. The producer is relieved because the deck might help with stakeholder buy-in. The tech lead is uneasy but stays quiet. The art lead is excited.

Two weeks later, the producer notices the same problems:

Design tasks are still a mix of experiments and "surely we'll need this."

Art is producing assets that might never ship because the core loop is still changing.

Engineering is building infrastructure "just in case."

The build feedback loop is slow because integration isn't treated as a priority.

Scope creep is creeping because nothing in the deck said "no" to anything.

The deck didn't fail because it was wrong. It failed because it was non-operational.

Why this happens (and why smart people repeat it)

This anti-pattern survives because it satisfies powerful psychological needs, especially under uncertainty.

First: it creates the *feeling* of alignment without the pain of alignment. Real alignment requires trade-offs. Trade-offs create friction. A deck can give you unity without conflict by staying abstract.

Second: it's politically safe. Slides are easier than saying "we are not doing this," "we must cut this," "we cannot afford that," or "this is the constraint stack." A deck lets leaders look decisive while avoiding the consequences of decisiveness.

Third: it protects identity. "Direction" in games is emotional. If the team admits the direction is still unknown, it feels like failure. A deck gives you an identity early: "this is who we are." Once that identity is attached, people resist the ugly work of turning it into shippable choices, because that work forces compromises.

Fourth: it's a communication shortcut, especially with publishers. You can sell a story faster than you can sell a decision system. The risk is believing that what sells also leads.

None of this requires bad intentions. It's a normal human response to ambiguity: replace uncertainty with narrative. The problem is that production doesn't run on narrative. It runs on decisions.

The tell: what's missing in a dead deck

A dead deck has strong adjectives and weak commitments.

It describes what the game "is" but not what the team will do when ideas conflict. It talks about pillars but doesn't rank them. It hints at constraints but doesn't define them. It shows features but doesn't define nongoals. It promises vibe and vision, but doesn't specify what wins next week.

In other words: it does not change behavior.

If you want a brutal but accurate test: if you can delete the deck and nothing in your planning changes, the deck was never a production tool.

How it damages the project (even when it looks harmless)

The first damage is subtle: it delays the moment of truth. Because everyone thinks "we have direction now," they stop pushing for explicit trade-offs. That means decisions stay soft longer, which increases rework later.

The second damage is cultural: it trains the team that words matter more than decisions. People learn that alignment means saying the right things, not doing the right cuts.

The third damage is operational: it creates parallel realities. Leadership refers to the deck. The team operates on the backlog. When those diverge, trust dies. Producers get blamed for "not executing the vision," and the team gets blamed for "not understanding direction," but the real issue is the bridge between vision and backlog was never built.

The fourth damage is external: publishers and stakeholders will eventually notice that the deck is not predictive. They will start managing you through oversight and approvals, because you've proven you can present clarity while operating in ambiguity.

How to tell if the deck is alive: a simple validation test

A clear test. Here it is. It takes minutes.

After a vision deck is "approved," you should be able to answer these questions immediately:

What are the top three decisions that the deck implies?
What are the top three things we will NOT do because of the deck?
What changes in the backlog this week because the deck exists?

If you can't answer these, the deck is dead. It may still be useful for selling, but it is not an alignment tool.

A second test, even simpler: pick any slide with a pillar statement and ask, "show me the backlog items that directly serve this pillar." If you can't trace it, you have decorative alignment.

How to "revive" a dead deck in 30 minutes

You don't fix this by making a better deck. You fix it by extracting decisions and forcing impact.

The fastest revival method is to convert the deck into a one-pager-level operating frame and then commit the implications into the backlog.

Step one: extract the pillars and rewrite them as operational rules. If a pillar is a vibe word, make it a testable statement. If you can't test it, it won't drive decisions.

Step two: define the constraint stack for the current phase. Time, runway/budget reality, build health/performance, platform assumptions, and content boundaries. Keep it short, but make it real.

Step three: write five nongoals for the phase. This is where scope creep dies. If your deck never says "no," it cannot protect the project.

Step four: choose one phase win condition. In pre-prod this is usually "validate the loop" or "validate the first hour." This turns the deck from a description into a plan for learning.

Step five: translate this into backlog impact. Not by writing tasks for everything. By doing three concrete moves:

Remove or freeze items that contradict nongoals.

Reprioritize items that validate the win condition.

Add explicit decision placeholders where the deck was vague (so you don't pretend they're decided).

At the end of 30 minutes, you don't need a new deck. You need one outcome: the backlog looks different. If it doesn't, nothing changed.

The balanced stance: decks are fine, but they must not pretend to be decisions

A vision deck can be a useful communication artifact. It can inspire. It can help sell. It can help onboard.

But if it doesn't produce trade-offs, it's not alignment. If it doesn't create nongoals, it's not scope control. If it doesn't change the backlog, it's not operational.

So the rule I'd give to any producer, creative lead, or CEO is simple:

Use a deck to tell the story.

Use a one-pager, pillars, constraints, and nongoals to run the project. And never confuse "everyone liked the slides" with "everyone knows what wins."

That confusion is expensive. And it's one of the easiest failure modes to avoid – if you insist that vision must cash out as decisions.

CHAPTER 3:
The Decision Contract
(decision rights, required inputs, escalation)

I. What a "Decision Contract" is and why it reduces stress (everyone knows how decisions happen)

If you're a producer, your job is not to "make people agree." Your job is to make decisions real, predictable, and survivable.

Most project stress doesn't come from hard work. It comes from **decision uncertainty**: people don't know what is decided, who decides, how decisions get made, and whether today's decision will still be true next week. That uncertainty creates shadow decisions, rework, defensive behavior, and the feeling that planning is theater.

A Decision Contract is the simplest antidote I know.

It's not a legal document. It's an operational rule: **a decision only exists if it follows an agreed minimal format, is owned, and is visible.**

That's it.

The problem it solves: "soft decisions" and invisible reality

In many teams, decisions happen in one of these ways:

A quick comment in chat.
A side conversation after a meeting.
A "sounds good" from someone senior.
A late review note that quietly overrides weeks of work.
A producer writes it down, but nobody treats it as binding.

From the producer's perspective, the result is always the same: the team works on assumptions, then discovers those assumptions were never shared or never committed. People feel blindsided. Work gets redone. Trust in plans collapses.

This is what I mean by shadow decisions: decisions that affect the project but don't exist in the open where execution lives.

A Decision Contract reduces stress because it kills the shadow layer. It forces the project to have one reality.

What a Decision Contract actually is

A Decision Contract is a lightweight protocol that answers, in a consistent way:

What was decided?
Who decided it?
Why now?
What trade-off did we accept?
What changes because of it?
How do we know it's committed (not just discussed)?
When do we revisit it, if ever?

It doesn't need to be long. It needs to be complete enough that nobody can later say "I didn't know" or "I thought it was still open."

The key concept is **commit signal**. Teams talk constantly. Discussion is cheap. Commitment is expensive. If you don't define what "committed" means, you get endless half-decisions that create stress without creating progress.

Why it reduces stress specifically (mechanically, not emotionally)

Stress drops when the system becomes predictable.

A Decision Contract reduces stress in three mechanical ways.

First, it reduces rework. Most rework is not caused by learning. It's caused by decisions that weren't real. A contract makes decisions real earlier.

Second, it reduces social anxiety. People stop guessing what leadership wants. They stop optimizing for politics. They stop holding back work "until we're sure." That alone increases throughput.

Third, it protects the producer from becoming the "human router" of every decision. Without a contract, producers end up carrying project reality in their heads and trying to keep everyone synchronized manually. That doesn't scale. A contract externalizes reality into a shared artifact.

When everyone knows how decisions happen, fewer people feel the need to "secure" decisions privately. Shadow decisions become unnecessary because the official path is fast and trusted.

The intended environment: one direction owner, many contributors

You said the typical setup is one strong owner of direction. That's common and it can work very well – if the system around that owner is healthy.

The Decision Contract is not about limiting the direction owner. It's about preventing them from unintentionally destabilizing production.

In a one-owner model, the two biggest risks are:

Drive-by decisions: the owner reacts late, without seeing the full blast radius.

Decision ambiguity: the owner speaks, but nobody knows if it was a thought, a preference, or a command.

A contract solves both by making each high-impact decision pass through the same small gate: explicitly stated, explicitly traded off, explicitly committed, and explicitly broadcast.

This also makes the owner's authority more effective. When decisions are clear and durable, the team can execute faster. Authority stops being "constant intervention" and becomes "stable direction."

What decisions require a contract

Not every choice needs a contract. If you force everything through it, it becomes bureaucracy and people will route around it.

The contract is for decisions that create expensive ripple effects. You identified three categories: scope, pillars, and quality. That's a strong, clean set.

Scope decisions: adding/removing features, changing deliverables, changing milestone content.
Pillar decisions: redefining what "wins," changing the priorities that guide trade-offs.
Quality decisions: changing the bar, accepting debt, choosing where "good enough" is allowed.

These are the decisions that, if made informally, generate weeks of confusion and rework.

The structure: minimal fields that make a decision real

Let's describe the structure, not to dump a full template yet, so here is the minimum set of fields and why each exists.

Decision: the statement that is true after the decision. No hedging language.
Owner: the person accountable for the decision. In your model, often the direction owner for pillars, producer for scope packaging, and leads for domain constraints.
Why now: what changed or what evidence triggered it. This prevents random volatility.
Trade-off: what loses because of this decision. This is where fantasy dies.
Impact: what areas/backlog items are affected. Not exhaustive, but enough to prevent surprises.
Commit signal: how we know it's committed (e.g., one-pager updated + backlog updated + communicated).
Revisit rule: either "no revisit" for this phase, or a specific condition/date that triggers review.

That's it. If those fields exist, the decision is actionable and durable.

Notice what's missing: long justification, politics, detailed implementation. The contract is not a design doc. It's a decision anchor.

The formal rule (the one that actually changes behavior)

You wanted "formal rules." Here's the one that matters most, stated plainly:

If it changes scope, pillars, or the quality bar, and it does not exist as a Decision Contract, it is not a decision.

That may feel strict. It's supposed to. The strictness is the whole point. It eliminates the gray zone where stress grows.

You don't need punishments. The enforcement mechanism is simpler: the producer does not update plans or backlog based on non-contract statements. "Sounds good" is treated as discussion until it becomes a contract entry.

This forces people – especially high-authority people – to make decisions in a way the system can digest.

Where it lives and how it flows

A Decision Contract should live in one obvious place the whole team can access: a decision log linked from the one-pager, milestone brief, or your main project hub. If people can't find it in 10 seconds, it won't be used.

The flow should be equally simple:

A decision is proposed.
The owner commits it through the contract fields.
The producer ensures the commit signal is completed: one-pager/backlog updated, decision visible.
The team executes without guessing.

This is where stress reduction happens: execution stops depending on memory, proximity, and politics.

How it prevents shadow decisions and priority chaos

Shadow decisions survive because they're fast. So your contract process must also be fast. If it takes hours, people will route around it.

The correct target is: high-impact decisions should be capturable in a few minutes, because the structure is minimal. The producer's job is to make it easy to do the right thing.

Priority chaos is similar. The contract forces trade-offs. Every time someone tries to add, the system asks: "what do we remove?" That's how priorities become real. Not by repeating the word "priority," but by paying for changes.

The payoff for a producer

A good Decision Contract system gives you something rare: the ability to plan without pretending.

Plans become more stable because decisions become durable.
Rework drops because decisions are visible and committed.
Stakeholder conversations improve because you can show an explicit decision trail.
Team stress drops because nobody has to guess what reality is.

And the direction owner benefits too: they get fewer "why did we build this?" surprises, fewer last-minute rescues, and more consistent execution of their intent.

A Decision Contract isn't paperwork. It's the minimum structure required for a team to move fast without lying to itself.

II. Roles and decision rights: decider / recommender / contributor / informed (simple, not corporate)

Decision chaos rarely comes from "bad decisions." It comes from unclear decision rights.

In a 30–100 person team, ambiguity is expensive. People can't "just talk to everyone." Informal alignment breaks down. The same topic gets debated in five places, and the outcome depends on who was in the room. That creates shadow decisions, rework, and stress.

You don't need corporate bureaucracy to fix this. You need one simple rule: **for any decision that matters, everyone should know who decides, who recommends, who contributes, and who must be informed.**

This is basically a lean, useful version of RACI – without the corporate vibe.

Why this matters (especially at 30–100)

At this scale, you'll hit these predictable failure modes if decision rights are vague:

- Multiple people believe they're the decider, so decisions stall or get reversed.
- Nobody believes they're the decider, so decisions never become real.
- Contributors try to "win" by lobbying in private, because the formal path is unclear or slow.
- Producers become human routers, trying to keep everyone synced manually.
- Backlog becomes a battlefield of half-decisions and unpriced requests.

Decision rights are the antidote because they make decision-making predictable. Predictability reduces stress. People can disagree, but they stop guessing how reality will be formed.

The four roles (minimal, operational definitions)

Keep these definitions tight. The moment you add nuance, you lose the point.

Decider

The person who makes the call when trade-offs exist. One decider per decision. Not a group. Not "the leads." A single accountable owner.

The decider's job is not to be the smartest person in the room. It's to make a decision that fits the project frame: pillars, constraints, and current win condition.

If there are two deciders, you have no decider.

Recommender

The person responsible for bringing a clear recommendation, including options and trade-offs. The recommender does the thinking work so the decider doesn't have to improvise.

A strong recommender does not bring a pile of information. They bring a proposed choice and the cost of each alternative.

Contributor

Someone whose input materially affects the quality of the decision. Contributors supply constraints, risks, implementation realities, and second-order effects.

Contributors are not "everyone who has an opinion." They are the people whose domain will be impacted, or who will carry the consequences.

Informed

People who must know the decision because it affects coordination, but who are not part of making the decision.

"Informed" is not a courtesy list. It's about preventing surprises and aligning execution.

A practical test: if someone needs to change their work because of this decision, they must be informed quickly.

The producer's role (process owner, not the decider)

Let me emphasize this strongly, so I'll state it plainly: **the producer owns the decision process, not necessarily the decision outcome.**

In many teams, producers are forced into being deciders because nobody else will commit. That's unhealthy unless it's explicitly the producer's domain (often scope packaging and milestone delivery).

A healthy setup looks like this:

- The producer ensures the decision exists in a Decision Contract format.
- The producer ensures the right recommender and contributors are involved.
- The producer ensures the decision has an explicit trade-off and backlog impact.
- The producer ensures visibility: the informed group actually gets informed.

This is what makes the system scale. Without it, decisions are either slow (too many people) or chaotic (too few rules).

How this maps to your key decision types (scope, pillars, budget)

You wanted examples in these three areas, so here's how the roles typically make sense in a 30–100 team where domain deciders can exist.

Scope decisions (what ships in the milestone / what gets cut)

Decider: often the producer *or* a direction owner, depending on your org.

Recommender: producer (because they see the plan, dependencies, and milestone pressure).

Contributors: leads impacted by the cut/add (design, tech, art, QA).

Informed: the whole team affected by priority changes.

The important part is that scope decisions require explicit trade-offs. If scope decisions don't have a clear decider, you get endless "just one more thing."

Pillar decisions (what 'wins' / what the game is optimizing for)

Decider: direction owner (game director/creative owner) in most cases.

Recommender: can be design lead or producer depending on where the evidence is coming from (playtests, market feedback, constraints).

Contributors: tech lead (feasibility), art lead (production implications), producer (constraints/runway).

Informed: everyone, because pillars change how work should be judged.

Pillars are high-leverage. If you let them drift through committee, they become vague. If you let them change through drive-by feedback, you destabilize the whole project.

Budget/runway decisions (what we can afford, what we must de-risk)

Decider: typically project owner/producer/leadership – depends on company structure, but it must be explicit.

Recommender: producer (burn, milestone dependencies, delivery risk), sometimes finance/ops if present.

Contributors: leads who can propose cheaper alternatives (scope reduction, tech risk reduction, content caps).

Informed: leads at minimum; often broader team at a high level if it affects staffing/scope.

The key here is clarity. Budget decisions made in secrecy tend to create late panic cuts. Budget decisions made with no process tend to create fantasy scope.

The common failure modes (and how the roles prevent them)

This simple model is mainly to prevent predictable traps:

- **Decider by absence:** nobody commits, so the decision "happens" through drift.
- **Decider by loudness:** the most forceful person becomes the decider informally.
- **Recommender without responsibility:** people bring problems, not recommendations.
- **Contributor overload:** too many contributors = slow decisions and diluted accountability.
- **Informed too late:** people discover decisions through changed tasks, causing resentment and rework.

If you assign these four roles clearly, most of these failure modes disappear without adding meetings.

The minimum standard for "decision rights" in practice

To keep this simple and usable: for any decision that touches **scope, pillars, or budget**, you should be able to answer in one breath:

“Decider is X, recommender is Y, contributors are A/B/C, informed are D.”

If you can’t, you’re gambling on coordination.

And once you have that, the Decision Contract from the previous topic becomes easy to enforce: the roles tell you who fills which parts of the contract, and the producer ensures it’s captured and translated into backlog impact.

This is how you scale decision-making without turning into a corporate machine: clear rights, minimal roles, visible outcomes.

III. Required decision inputs: options, costs, risks, impact on pillars/constraints, alternatives

A decision is only as good as the inputs it's fed.

Most teams don't fail because the decider is incompetent. They fail because the decision arrives with missing context, hidden costs, and vague trade-offs. Then the decider either delays (because it's unsafe), or commits blindly (because there's pressure). Both outcomes create stress and rework.

This topic is about a simple standard: **certain inputs are required before a decision is allowed to "exist."** Not because we love process, but because it prevents two common killers: shadow decisions and priority chaos.

And yes – at team scale, the producer is the natural owner of this standard. Not because the producer should be the decider, but because the producer is the person who protects decision quality, decision visibility, and backlog impact.

Why "required inputs" reduce chaos

When inputs are incomplete, decisions become emotional. People argue based on taste, status, or fear. Nobody can quantify cost or risk, so "winning" becomes persuasion.

Required inputs shift the conversation from persuasion to trade-offs.

They also make decision-making faster. That sounds counterintuitive, but it's true in practice: a decider can decide quickly when options are clear, costs are priced, and risks are named. They stall when they have to assemble the decision themselves from scattered opinions.

Finally, required inputs create fairness. Not "everyone gets a vote," but "everyone knows what information is needed for a decision to be valid." That predictability is a stress reducer.

The producer's job: make decisions safe to make

In a healthy team, the producer doesn't walk into a review asking "so… what do we do?" The producer walks in with a structured choice that can be decided.

That structure is the required inputs standard.

Producers enforce it in two ways:

First, they refuse to treat a decision as real unless the required inputs exist. This is not stubbornness. It's protecting the project from soft decisions that cause rework.

Second, they make it easy for recommenders and contributors to provide those inputs consistently, without needing a big ritual every time.

This is where flexibility matters. Some teams will use a half-page brief for major choices. Others will use a small template in a ticket or doc. The standard should scale with decision size, but the core inputs stay the same.

What inputs are required (and why)

For decisions that affect scope, pillars, or quality bar, you want a minimum set that consistently forces trade-offs into daylight.

Options
At least two options whenever possible. If you only present one option, you're not requesting a decision – you're requesting approval.

A useful baseline is "do nothing" or "keep current course," even if it's obviously bad. It gives you a reference point and prevents false urgency.

Costs
Cost means real cost: time, people, integration, QA surface, opportunity cost. Not just "it's a week." In games, the hidden cost is often retesting and downstream churn.

Producers don't need perfect estimates. They need cost ranges and relative sizing: "small/medium/large," plus the shape of cost (one-time vs recurring).

Risks
Every option has risk. If someone claims an option is low-risk, they usually mean they haven't looked.

Name the failure mode: what can go wrong and how you'll detect it early. "Risk" without a failure mode is just fear.

Impact on pillars / constraints

This is the alignment hook. Every option should clearly state which pillar it serves (or violates) and which constraints it stresses.

If you can't connect an option to pillars, it's likely scope creep or local optimization. If you can't connect it to constraints, it's likely fantasy.

Alternatives (including hybrids)

This is where good producers earn their keep. A lot of conflicts are framed as false binaries: "we either do A or B." In reality, there's often a smaller alternative that preserves the pillar outcome without paying full cost.

Alternatives can be "smaller version," "phase it," "fake it," "cut adjacent scope to pay for it," or "change the success criteria."

The point is not to generate infinite options. The point is to show the decider that you explored the possibility space and found the least-worst choice.

How many options is "enough"?

For small decisions, **two options** is enough: proposed vs baseline.
For larger decisions, **two plus an alternative** is usually the sweet spot.
For very high-impact decisions, you can go to three real options, but only if you can still compare them cleanly.

If you present five options, you're often avoiding responsibility. The decider will either pick randomly or ask you to come back with fewer.

A mature recommender brings a recommendation, not a buffet.

The decision-input anti-cheats (the common lies)

These are patterns that create chaos because they bypass trade-offs.

False binary

"We either ship this feature or the game fails." Usually wrong. Often a lack of alternatives work.

Approval disguised as a decision

One option presented as "the decision," with no baseline, no cost, no risk. That's politics, not decision-making.

No priced cost

"It shouldn't take long." Translation: nobody wants to own the estimate. This is how "small changes" become slow death.

Risk handwaving

"Engineering will figure it out." "QA will cover it." "We'll optimize later." That's not mitigation. That's kicking the can into crunch.

Pillar laundering

Labeling a preference as "pillar-aligned" without explaining how it improves the player outcome. If "pillar" becomes a weapon, it loses value.

Hidden scope

An option that looks cheap because it excludes integration, tooling, content updates, tutorials, localization, platform requirements, or long-tail maintenance.

No backlog impact stated

"We can do this" without saying what stops. This is how teams accumulate work until time collapses.

A producer should treat these as red flags. Not to shame people, but to protect the system.

How to keep this simple and non-corporate

The fear is always: "this will become paperwork."

It won't if you enforce two principles:

One: scale the detail to the decision size. A major pillar change deserves a half-page brief. A small scope cut might be three paragraphs in a ticket.

Two: treat the output as operational. If it doesn't change backlog priorities, it's not a real decision brief. It's commentary.

The structure is minimal because it is designed to be used, not admired.

A copyable "Decision Input Sheet" (adapt it)

Use this as a lightweight standard. You can paste it into a ticket, a doc, or a decision log entry. Change headings to fit your team. Keep the intent.

Decision title:
Decision type: Scope / Pillars / Quality (or other)
Owner (decider):
Recommender:
Why now (trigger / evidence):

Options (include baseline):
A) ______
B) ______
(Optional C) ______

Costs (rough ranges, incl. integration/QA):
A) ______
B) ______
C) ______

Risks (failure modes + early signals):
A) ______
B) ______
C) ______

Impact on pillars / constraints:
Which pillar(s) does each option support or violate?
Which constraints does it stress (time, build health, perf, content caps, platform)?

Alternatives / hybrids considered:
What smaller versions or phased approaches were considered, and why rejected?

Backlog impact (what changes):
What gets cut, delayed, or deprioritized if we pick option A/B/C?

Recommendation:
Which option you recommend and why (one paragraph, not a novel).

This is intentionally adaptable. The only non-negotiable part is that the brief forces options, cost, risk, pillar/constraint impact, and backlog consequences into the open.

The producer's enforcement rule

To make this standard actually reduce stress, you need one clear norm:

If a decision affects scope, pillars, or quality bar, and it does not have these inputs, it is not ready to decide.

That sounds strict. It's also kinder than letting the team drift into shadow decisions and chaos. Because once the decision is made, people build on it. And if the foundation is soft, you'll pay for it with rework and burnout.

Required inputs are not bureaucracy. They are how you keep decisions safe, repeatable, and aligned – so your team can execute without guessing.

IV. Rule: "who can say NO" vs "who can say YES"

Most scope creep isn't created by malice. It's created by an asymmetry. Everyone can say "yes" to ideas. Almost nobody can say "no" in a way that sticks.

So the backlog grows, the milestone becomes fantasy, and the project "solves" it later with crunch, panic cuts, or quality collapse. Then everyone acts surprised.

If you want to protect scope, you need a simple rule that makes approval harder than refusal:

NO is a safety stop. YES is a commitment that must pass a gate.

That's the whole idea.

In a domain-decider model, this becomes powerful because it respects expertise. Domain owners can stop the train when their domain is about to be overloaded. But adding work ("yes") requires a process that forces trade-offs and keeps the project coherent.

The core distinction (and why it matters)

A "NO" is not a decision outcome. It's a control mechanism.

When someone with the right decision rights says NO, they are not claiming "this will never happen." They are saying: "we are not accepting this change into the plan without paying for it."

That's why you chose: NO stops until a trade-off exists.

A "YES" is fundamentally different. YES creates obligations: more work, more integration, more QA surface, more risk. In production, "yes" is expensive. Which means "yes" must be harder.

If your team treats YES as cheap and NO as rude, you will drift into chaos even with good people.

The anti-pattern you want to kill

Here's the classic failure mode:

Everyone can say YES:

- the creative owner likes the idea,
- the designer wants to try it,
- art sees an opportunity,
- tech says "we can probably do it,"
- marketing gets excited,
- someone promises it externally "just as a stretch."

But nobody can say NO in a binding way. Or if they do, it's seen as negativity that will be "worked around."

What happens next is deterministic:

- the idea gets added "small," without a trade-off;
- it expands through hidden dependencies;
- the plan silently breaks;
- the team pays with overtime, rework, and stress.

This is how scope creep becomes the default operating mode. Not because people are careless, but because the system rewards YES and punishes NO.

The healthier rule set for a domain-decider team

You said: domain deciders exist, and the producer's job is to ensure coherence. Good. Here's how this works in practice without turning into bureaucracy.

Who can say NO?

Domain deciders can say NO when a request violates their domain constraints or breaks the current phase frame.

Examples:

- Tech can say NO when a change breaks build health, performance budgets, or introduces high-risk architecture late.
- Art can say NO when a request breaks pipeline reality, asset budgets, or requires rework that cannot be absorbed.

- QA/release can say NO when a change increases test surface beyond capacity, or endangers stability/ship readiness.
- Production can say NO when a request is unpriced scope: no trade-off, no plan impact, no owner.

The crucial detail: NO is not "I don't like it." NO is "this is unsafe to accept into the plan."

Who can say YES?

YES is not owned by a person. It's owned by a gate.

In other words: *any* YES that affects milestone scope must satisfy conditions. If it doesn't, it isn't a YES. It's a suggestion.

You can still have a direction owner who ultimately decides, but the system should force the decision to be expensive enough that random YES does not slip through.

What "YES requires a process" actually means

To protect scope, your YES gate must enforce three things:

First: it must name the trade-off. If we add this, what do we remove or delay? If nothing is removed, it's not approved scope. It's scope creep.

Second: it must fit the alignment frame. Which pillar does it serve? Which constraint does it stress? If you can't answer, it's likely not aligned, or it's too early to commit.

Third: it must be visible. A "yes" in a DM is not a yes. A "yes" without backlog impact is not a yes. A "yes" without a Decision Contract entry (for scope-class decisions) is not a yes.

This is where the producer "watch." The producer doesn't decide the creative direction, but they enforce that approvals are real: priced, recorded, translated into plan.

A clear, readable set of examples

Let's make it concrete with three common scope situations.

1) "Small feature" added to the milestone

Someone says: "This is just a small change. It will make the game better."

A domain NO can stop this immediately: "No, not as-is. It's not priced and it expands QA surface."

A YES requires the gate: a short decision input sheet with two options (do it vs don't), rough costs, risks, impact on pillars/constraints, and – most importantly – what gets cut. If the proposer can't name the cut, the request doesn't get in.

2) "Polish later" promise that quietly grows scope

Someone says: "We'll do it in polish," but the "it" is actually a design change that affects multiple systems.

NO should trigger here because "polish later" is often code for "we refuse to decide now." A domain decider can stop the ambiguity: "No commitment without defining success criteria and blast radius."

YES can still happen, but only in the right phase and only with an explicit quality bar change: what is good enough now, and what is deferred intentionally – recorded, not implied.

3) "Can we just add one more platform / mode / variation?"

Even when you want it, it's scope explosives disguised as a checkbox.

NO is valid until you have a constraint-aware plan: budget/runway impact, staffing impact, and what gets removed. If the answer is "we'll manage," that's not a plan.

YES requires explicit re-scoping. If you can't afford the cut, you can't afford the yes.

These examples look strict, but they're actually respectful. They respect people's time and protect the team from silent commitments.

How to phrase NO so it's firm without being toxic

A lot of teams avoid NO because they associate it with negativity. You can solve that with language that anchors NO in the system, not in personal preference.

A good NO sounds like:

"I'm saying no to accepting this into the plan without a trade-off. Bring it back with cost, risk, and what we cut."

This keeps the door open while still protecting scope.

Also: don't make NO a debate. NO is a stop sign. Debate happens after the stop, when you price the change.

The producer's enforcement role (the part most teams miss)

This rule only works if someone enforces the distinction between talk and commitment.

The producer's job is to protect the gate:

- If it's a scope-impacting YES without a trade-off, it doesn't enter the backlog as committed work.
- If a domain NO is raised, it pauses intake until the decision is re-framed with trade-offs.
- When a YES is approved, the producer ensures it is translated into backlog impact immediately.

Without this, the system degrades into "we say we have rules, but we bypass them when it's inconvenient." That's worse than having no rules, because it destroys trust.

The payoff: fewer "yeses," more real progress

When NO is a safety stop and YES is a priced commitment, three things happen:

You add less scope, but you ship more.
Decisions become predictable, which reduces stress.
The team stops relying on heroics to reconcile fantasy plans.

Scope creep doesn't die because people stop having ideas. It dies because the system stops accepting ideas for free.

V. Escalation: when to escalate, to whom, and in what format (without turning it into politics)

Escalation is not a failure. It's a safety system.

In a healthy project, escalation is how you prevent three things from quietly killing you: decision deadlocks, scope creep that bypasses trade-offs, and quality erosion that becomes permanent.

In an unhealthy project, escalation becomes politics: lobbying, CC-the-boss, weaponized urgency, and "I'll go over your head." That's when escalation stops being a safety system and starts being a power game.

The difference is not intention. The difference is whether escalation follows a clear process that everyone trusts.

The core rule: escalate problems, not people

If escalation feels personal, it will be avoided until it's too late – or abused as a weapon.

So the rule is simple: escalation is about **risk to the project frame** (pillars, constraints, scope/quality), not about who is right.

A producer's job is to keep it framed that way. When you escalate, you're not saying "X is blocking." You're saying "we have a decision that cannot be resolved at the current level without violating our frame or timeline."

When to escalate (and when not to)

You picked three triggers: deadlock, scope creep, quality. Good. These are exactly the ones that rot a project if left unresolved.

Escalate when you have a decision deadlock that blocks progress.

Not "we disagree." Disagreement is normal. Deadlock is when the team cannot choose an option and work is stalled, or worse – people start working in different directions.

A practical threshold: if a decision blocks execution for more than a short, agreed window (often 24–72 hours depending on cadence), you escalate. Not because you want authority, but because the cost of waiting is now higher than the cost of deciding with imperfect info.

Escalate when scope creep is attempting to enter without paying a trade-off.

This is where your "who can say NO vs who can say YES" rule should kick in. Escalation happens when someone tries to bypass the gate: sneak work into the backlog, promise it externally, or treat "small change" as free.

You don't escalate every request. You escalate the *pattern*: repeated unpriced changes, unclear ownership, or pressure to accept additions without cuts. That's not a feature discussion anymore. That's an integrity problem in your decision system.

Escalate when quality is being degraded in a way that will become structural.

Quality erosion is tricky because it often looks rational in the moment: "we'll fix it later," "we need to hit the milestone," "this is good enough."

Sometimes that's true. But if "good enough" is being used as a blanket excuse, you'll ship a broken product or you'll pay in a late crunch debt spiral.

Escalate when the quality compromise violates a pillar, breaks a constraint (like build stability), or creates recurring debt that will be paid with stress later.

The principle is consistent: escalation triggers when local optimization threatens global alignment.

To whom you escalate (the clean escalation chain)

In the model you're using, you have domain deciders, a producer as process owner, and a direction owner at the top of product intent. That's enough to build a clean chain that avoids politics.

Start at the lowest level that can actually resolve the trade-off. Escalation should move *up* only when the current level cannot decide without crossing into someone else's authority or into project-wide priorities.

A healthy chain looks like this:

Domain conflict or domain constraint issue -> domain deciders attempt resolution using pillars/constraints -> if they cannot converge, it goes to the producer as the process owner to reframe the decision properly (options, costs, risks, backlog impact) -> if the conflict is truly a product-level trade-off (pillars, scope packaging, quality bar), it goes to the direction owner as the decider -> only if it involves funding, contractual publisher commitments, or business-level constraints, it goes to exec/publisher-facing leadership.

The producer's role in the middle is critical. Without it, escalation becomes "who has more authority." With it, escalation stays "what decision must be made, with what trade-offs."

Also important: escalation is not a shortcut around decision rights. If a domain decider has a legitimate NO based on constraints, you don't bypass them. You escalate only to resolve the trade-off explicitly, not to override expertise casually.

In what format (and why format matters)

Escalation fails when it's just emotion delivered to authority. It succeeds when it is a structured choice.

So the format should match the urgency and the complexity, but the content must always be the same at its core: options, costs, risks, impact on pillars/constraints, and backlog trade-off.

There are two practical formats:

Asynchronous escalation (written brief) is best when:

- the decision is complex enough that people need time to think,
- you want to remove performative debate,
- the project is distributed across time zones,
- or you want a decision trail that reduces later confusion.

Synchronous escalation (short meeting) is best when:

- the decision blocks progress immediately,
- the cost of delay is high,
- or miscommunication risk is high and you need fast alignment.

A good thesis to adopt: default to async for clarity, go sync only when time pressure or ambiguity demands it. This reduces politics because it removes "winning the room" dynamics.

Regardless of format, the producer should enforce a simple standard: escalation arrives as a decision-ready package, not as a complaint.

How to keep escalation from turning into politics

Politics appears when escalation becomes a way to win by authority instead of by trade-offs.

You prevent that by enforcing three rules.

First: **no bypassing.** If you escalate, you do it through the agreed chain unless there is an emergency safety issue. "Going around" is how trust collapses.

Second: **no weaponized urgency.** Urgency must be justified by impact, not by volume. "We need an answer now" is not a reason. "Work is blocked and we are burning capacity daily" is a reason. The producer's job is to translate urgency into cost.

Third: **no ambush escalation.** CC-the-boss is the classic anti-pattern: pull in authority without giving the current decider a chance to resolve it, usually to pressure an outcome. It's toxic. It also trains people to stop cooperating.

If escalation is needed, it should be visible and fair: the relevant deciders are aware, the framing is clear, and the decision is made on explicit trade-offs.

The escalation anti-patterns (name them so you can kill them)

Let me directly name them. Here are the ones that matter most.

Escalation as lobbying

People shop for an answer they like by escalating selectively. The cure is a single decision log and a single chain: escalation produces an official decision, not a private agreement.

Weaponized urgency

"Now or never" language used to skip trade-offs. The cure is the YES gate: no unpriced yes, no matter how urgent it feels.

CC-the-boss escalation

Pulling authority into a thread to pressure an outcome. The cure is process discipline: escalation requires the structured framing and the right participants.

Drive-by escalation

Dropping a problem on leadership without options, costs, or risks. The cure is required inputs: escalation is not allowed without a decision-ready package.

Escalation as punishment

Using escalation to shame or discredit someone. The cure is cultural and procedural: escalate risks and decisions, never personalities.

What good escalation looks like in practice

In a healthy project, escalation feels boring.

A producer says: "We have a decision deadlock / scope creep attempt / quality risk. Here are the options. Here are costs and risks. Here is how each option impacts pillars and constraints. Here is what we cut if we accept it. We need a decision by X because work is blocked."

The decider responds with a clear call. The one-pager and backlog are updated. The informed group is told. People go back to work without guessing.

That's the real purpose: escalation should *restore execution*, not create drama.

If escalation is currently political in a team, the fix is not "be nicer." The fix is to make escalation procedural: consistent chain, decision-ready framing, explicit trade-offs, and visible outcomes.

That is how you keep escalation as a safety system instead of a power game.

VI. Decision log: the minimal decision record (what, why, trade-off, owner, date, consequences)

If you want decisions to reduce stress, you need one thing: a shared memory that doesn't rely on people's heads.

That's what a decision log is.

Not a novel. Not a bureaucratic archive. A small, reliable record of the decisions that shape the project – so the team doesn't keep re-litigating the same topics, and so "shadow decisions" can't quietly rewrite reality.

A decision log is also the missing link between your one-pager (the frame) and your backlog (execution). The one-pager says what wins. The backlog is what you're doing. The decision log explains how you moved from one to the other, especially when trade-offs hurt.

The producer's stance: enough logging to prevent rework, not enough to create paperwork

You explicitly don't want paranoia. Good. A paranoid decision log becomes a performance of control and a tax on execution.

So the rule is: **log only decisions that have durable consequences** – the ones that will matter in a week, a month, or during a postmortem.

If a decision can be reversed tomorrow with no cost, don't log it. If a decision changes scope, pillars, quality bar, constraints, or milestone outcomes, log it. If a decision is likely to be questioned later, log it.

This keeps the log small enough to stay alive and valuable enough to be trusted.

Where it should live (choose availability over perfection)

You said: let the team choose. That's the right approach.

The best location is the one that meets four conditions: accessible, clear, used, and up to date. That can be a wiki page, a shared doc, a lightweight database tool, or even a markdown file in a repo. The tool matters less than the habit.

A decision log that is perfect but ignored is worse than a simple log that is used.

One important constraint, since you want lead-only directly: keep the log in a place leads actually open during work. If it's "somewhere else," it will rot.

Lead-only log, team-wide awareness (without flooding everyone)

Keeping the log lead-only can work well at 30–100 people. It prevents noise and keeps authorship disciplined. But the wider team still needs two things:

They need to know the log exists and what it's for – so decisions feel predictable, not arbitrary.

They need to see the outcomes of decisions that affect their work – so they aren't surprised through changed tasks.

A good operational pattern is: lead-only log + short broadcast of major decisions (the "what changed and what it means") with a link to the log entry. That keeps execution aligned without turning the log into a chatroom.

The minimal record: what fields must exist

A decision log entry is basically your Decision Contract captured after the fact in a consistent minimal format. You already named the core fields, and they're correct. Here is what each one is doing in the system.

What
The decision statement. One sentence. No hedging. It must be true after the decision.

Why
The trigger or evidence. This prevents "random volatility." It answers why we decided now.

Trade-off
What loses. This is the anti-scope-creep core. If trade-off is missing, you're logging a wish, not a decision.

Owner
The decider/accountable owner. This makes responsibility visible and prevents later "I thought someone else decided."

Date
Because context decays fast in production. Also because it helps you see decision churn.

Consequences
What this changes in practice: backlog changes, constraints updates, quality expectations, or follow-up actions. Consequences can be one sentence, or it can include links to epics/tickets if that's more useful in your setup.

That's the minimum that keeps the decision alive.

Everything else is optional. If you add too much, people stop writing entries.

How it connects to the rest of your system (without repeating it)

The one-pager is your stable frame. When a decision changes pillars, constraints, nongoals, or phase win condition, the one-pager must be updated – otherwise your frame and your log contradict each other.

Required decision inputs are what you use before the decision; the decision log is what you keep after. If the decision log is constantly missing costs/risks/trade-offs, that's a signal your input standard Is not being enforced.

Escalation becomes clean when a decision log exists, because escalation stops being "who said what" and becomes "which decision is blocked, what are the options, what is the trade-off."
And your "NO vs YES" rule becomes enforceable because every YES that changes scope should leave a trace: the trade-off and the consequences.

Three to five example entries (realistic and short)

Below are examples written in the minimal style. They're intentionally compact. You can expand them when a situation requires more detail.

1) Scope cut for milestone integrity

What: Cut Feature X from Milestone M to protect ship date and stability.
Why: Integration cost exceeded estimate; build stability trending down for 2 weeks.
Trade-off: Reduced player-facing variety in mid-game; marketing beat adjusted.
Owner: Producer (scope packaging) + Direction Owner (final call).
Date: 2026-12-03
Consequences: Epic "Feature X" moved to backlog backlog bucket "Post-M"; replace with smaller alternative Y. QA plan reduced by Z test cases. One-pager nongoals updated ("no new systems for M").

2) Pillar clarification (not a pivot, a sharpening)

What: Pillar P2 clarified to prioritize readability over mechanical complexity.
Why: Playtest feedback showed confusion spikes; onboarding time increased.
Trade-off: Some advanced mechanics postponed; depth shifted to mastery, not systems count.
Owner: Direction Owner.
Date: 2026-12-03
Consequences: Design backlog updated: remove mechanics expansion tasks, add readability/tuning tasks; art/UX alignment check scheduled; one-pager pillars updated.

3) Quality bar decision (intentional compromise)

What: Accept "good enough" animation fidelity for non-critical NPCs to protect performance budget.
Why: Performance on target hardware below budget; runtime spikes correlated with animation complexity.
Trade-off: Lower perceived polish in background characters; focus polish on first-hour experience.
Owner: Art Lead (recommendation) + Tech Lead (constraint) + Direction Owner (final call).
Date: 2026-12-03
Consequences: Update definition of done for NPCs; redirect animation time to hero characters; performance guardrail added to one-pager constraints.

4) Enforcing the YES gate (scope creep blocked)

What: Reject adding Feature Z to current milestone without a compensating cut.
Why: Request had no priced cost or trade-off; violates current nongoal ("no new core systems").
Trade-off: Feature Z deferred; stakeholder expectation managed explicitly.
Owner: Producer (process enforcement) + Direction Owner (final authority).
Date: 2026-12-03
Consequences: Feature Z captured as "candidate post-milestone" with required inputs; communicated "NO until trade-off" to team; no backlog change for current milestone.

5) Escalation resolution (deadlock closed)

What: Choose Option B for combat camera despite UX disagreement to protect stability and schedule.
Why: Deadlock blocked implementation; Option A carried high technical risk and unknown iteration cost.
Trade-off: Slightly less cinematic feel; regain predictability and testing speed.
Owner: Direction Owner after escalation.
Date: 2026-12-03
Consequences: Backlog updated to Option B tasks; camera prototype A stopped; follow-up review date set after next playtest to validate the trade.

These examples show the point: each entry is short, but it explains reality, trade-offs, and consequences.

A practical warning: don't let the log become a graveyard

Two failure modes kill decision logs.

One: it becomes too detailed, so people stop writing entries.
Two: it becomes too vague, so it stops being useful.

The fix is to keep the minimum fields strict, and let detail scale with risk. If a decision is controversial or expensive, add a bit more context and links. If it's straightforward, keep it tight.

Also: if the log is not updated within a short window after a major decision, it will be updated never. The habit matters more than the tool. In practice, the producer is usually the person who protects that habit.

What you get when this works

When the decision log is alive, you feel it immediately:

Fewer repeated debates.
Less "I didn't know" rework.
Cleaner escalation.
More stable planning.
Lower stress, because the team stops guessing what reality is.

It's one of the highest leverage "minimal process" tools you can implement – because it doesn't add work, it removes wasted work.

VII. Decision meetings: how to prep, how to timebox, how to avoid endless discussion

A "decision meeting" is not a special ceremony. It's a mode you can plug into whatever rhythm you already have: lead sync, planning, milestone review, even an ad-hoc call. What makes it a decision meeting is one thing: **you enter with a decision to make, and you leave with a decision or an explicit next step that makes the decision possible.**

Endless discussion happens when the meeting is trying to do three jobs at once: discover facts, resolve vision, and decide. That's why you identified the real culprits: missing data, missing decider, and missing vision. If you don't control those, timeboxes don't help – people will just spill over.

So the producer's job is to make the decision safe to make: clarify who decides, get the minimum inputs, and frame the choice against pillars/constraints. Then a timebox becomes real.

The producer's baseline rule: no decision without a decider and a decision shape

Before you put a decision into a meeting, you should be able to say:
Who is the decider?
What is the decision question (one sentence)?
What are the options (at least baseline vs proposed)?
What trade-off is on the table?

If any of those are missing, you don't have a decision meeting. You have a discussion meeting. That's fine sometimes, but don't pretend it will produce a decision.

This is the fastest way to kill "no decider" and half of "no vision" problems: if the owner is present, and the question is framed in terms of pillars/constraints, the room can converge.

Prep: "async-first" without turning it into homework

You're right: people should be at least head-up before the call. The trick is to keep prep small and consistent.

For any decision that affects scope, pillars, or quality bar, use the same minimal pre-read shape (based on the required inputs you already established): options, costs, risks, pillar/constraint impact, and backlog trade-off.

The producer sends this in advance in a place everyone will see, with one clear ask: "Come prepared to choose between A and B; if you propose C, you must name what we cut."

That's enough. You don't need a long doc. The pre-read's job is to prevent the meeting from being used to discover basic facts.

This directly addresses your biggest endless-discussion trigger: missing data. If the data isn't available, the pre-read should say so explicitly and propose what data is needed and by when. Otherwise you will "discuss" uncertainty until the timebox runs out.

The minimal meeting set: keep the room small on purpose

You said: leads plus owner. That's a good default for decisions that change the project frame.

The rule is: the meeting includes the decider, the recommender (often the producer), and only the contributors who materially affect the trade-off. Everyone else gets informed after.

If you invite observers, they will either stay silent and waste time, or they will participate and dilute accountability. Both increase discussion time.

The producer protects the room size not because they like control, but because small rooms decide; large rooms negotiate.

Timeboxing that actually works

A timebox is not "we stop talking at 30 minutes." It's "we are forcing the conversation through a structure that produces an outcome within 30 minutes."

For most production decisions, these timeboxes work well:

- 15 minutes for small scope/priority calls (when inputs are clear).
- 30 minutes for normal cross-domain trade-offs.
- 45 minutes for high-impact, high-ambiguity decisions where the decider is present and the pre-read exists.

If you go beyond 45 minutes, you're usually in one of two states: either you're missing information, or you're missing alignment frame (pillars/constraints). Longer meetings rarely fix either. They just make people tired, and tired people don't make good decisions.

A producer-friendly rule that keeps things honest:

If the decision can't be made within the timebox, the meeting must end with one of these outcomes:

- "Postpone with a defined data request and owner," or
- "Escalate," or
- "Decide a temporary rule for the next period," if the real decision requires evidence.

The worst outcome is "we'll think about it" with no next step. That is how discussion becomes endless.

An agenda skeleton (minutes) you can reuse

This is the practical structure that prevents the meeting from drifting into philosophy.

0–3 min: State the decision and the decider

Producer: "Decision today is X. Decider is Y. We're choosing between A and B. We leave with a call or a defined next step."

This alone fixes half of "no decider" and keeps the room honest.

3–8 min: Present options and baseline, with trade-offs

Recommender (often producer or lead): "Option A costs..., risks..., impacts pillars/constraints..., requires cutting... Option B ... Baseline is ..."

No debate yet. Just clarity.

8–15 min: Questions only to close factual gaps

This is where you control "missing data." Questions must be about facts that change the choice, not about taste.

If a critical fact is unknown, you flag it explicitly: "We can't decide without X; owner is Z; due date is D."

15–25 min: Debate the trade-off, anchored to pillars/constraints

This is where vision confusion often shows up. The producer keeps it anchored: "Which pillar wins here? Which constraint are we protecting? What is the phase win condition?"

If the room starts arguing about vision, that's a signal your one-pager/pillars are too vague or not trusted. You don't solve that in this meeting by re-writing the game. You either clarify the pillar in a follow-up, or you decide using the current frame and log the risk.

25–30 min: Decision + commit signal

Decider makes the call. Producer immediately states the commitment mechanics: "We will update backlog by today, update one-pager if needed, and log the decision."

This prevents the classic failure where a decision is "made" but never becomes real.

You can compress or expand this, but keep the shape. The shape is what kills endless discussion.

How to avoid endless discussion (the producer's intervention patterns)

Most endless meetings don't need better facilitation. They need stronger constraints on what is allowed to happen in the room.

Here are the practical interventions that work without sounding corporate. Use them as patterns, not scripts.

When discussion drifts into opinion without trade-offs:
Producer: "What do we cut to pay for this? If we can't name the cut, we're not deciding, we're wishing."

When there's no decider behavior (everyone debating as if it's committee):
Producer: "We're collecting input. The call belongs to X. Let's give them clear options and costs."

When vision is unclear and people debate "what the game is":
Producer: "This is a pillar/frame question. Are we comfortable deciding

under the current pillars, or do we need a dedicated re-alignment step? If the latter, we define what needs to be clarified and by when."

When data is missing and the room keeps looping:
Producer: "We don't have the data to decide. Who owns getting it, and when? Until then, what's the safe default?"

When someone tries to introduce a new option late (common derail):
Producer: "Option C is valid, but it needs the same inputs: cost, risk, pillar impact, and trade-off. If we can't price it now, we log it and decide between A and B today."

When the meeting becomes a history lesson ("why we got here"):
Producer: "Noted. For today, we need a forward decision. If root cause matters, we schedule it separately."

These interventions are not about being strict. They're about protecting the team from spending time without producing reality.

The key to timeboxing: decisions must create backlog impact immediately

Endless discussion often continues after the meeting because the decision never lands in the backlog. People keep debating because reality didn't change.

So the producer closes the loop: once the decision is made, it must immediately trigger backlog changes and, if relevant, one-pager updates and a decision log entry.

This is also how you prevent "no vision" problems from becoming permanent. If the pillar is vague, decisions will expose it. Log it as a frame gap and schedule a re-alignment update. That's how the system improves over time rather than repeating the same debates.

What "good" looks like

A good decision meeting feels almost disappointingly simple:

Everyone knew the question coming in.
Options and trade-offs were visible.
The decider made a call within the timebox.

The decision became real through backlog updates and logging. Disagreement was allowed, but looping was not.

That's what reduces stress: not fewer hard decisions, but fewer ambiguous non-decisions that waste time and create rework.

VIII. Anti-patterns: consensus theater, surprise veto, "no one decides, but everyone has an opinion"

These three anti-patterns look different on the surface, but they're the same disease: **decision ambiguity disguised as collaboration**.

They waste time, increase stress, and create rework because they replace a predictable decision system with social guessing games.

To make this practical, I'll use one guiding scenario and show how it mutates into each anti-pattern – and how to counter it using the tools you already established in this chapter: decision rights, Decision Contract, decision log, and escalation.

The guiding scenario: "Project Helix" and the meeting that never ends

Project Helix is mid-production. Team size is around 60. There's a direction owner, multiple domain leads, and a producer trying to keep a milestone stable.

A problem appears: the core combat loop feels readable but "flat." Design wants to add a stamina system and new enemy behaviors. Tech warns about performance and systemic risk. Art is already behind on content. QA is seeing stability regressions. The milestone date is real.

This is a good moment for a real decision: do we expand mechanics, or do we deepen what we have? What do we cut to pay for it? Who decides?

Instead, Helix drifts into the three anti-patterns.

Anti-pattern 1: Consensus theater

Consensus theater is when the team pretends they are deciding together, but nobody is actually authorized – or willing – to make a call.

It looks polite and sounds collaborative, but burns hours and produces nothing.

In Helix, the producer calls a "discussion meeting." Everyone attends. Everyone speaks. People say "I'm aligned" and "this makes sense" because disagreeing feels risky and exhausting. The direction owner doesn't want to be the bad guy, so they keep the decision open: "Let's explore."

After the meeting, different people walk away with different interpretations:

- Design thinks stamina is approved "in principle."
- Tech thinks it's "a research spike."
- Art thinks it's "not happening this milestone."
- Producer thinks "we'll decide next week."

Meanwhile, work starts anyway – because the project doesn't stop. This is where rework is born.

Why it's toxic

Consensus theater feels safe because it avoids conflict in the room. But it exports conflict into the schedule, where it becomes expensive and personal.

It also trains the team that meetings exist to signal agreement, not to create reality.

How to recognize it

If after a decision meeting you cannot answer "what did we decide, what did we cut, and who owns it," you did not have alignment. You had theater.

Counter: make decision rights explicit, then enforce the Decision Contract gate

The antidote is simple:

- Start the meeting by naming the decider and the decision question.
- Require at least baseline vs proposed option.
- Require a trade-off before anything is treated as approved.
- Log the decision and update backlog immediately.

This is exactly what your Decision Contract and required inputs are for. They turn "discussion" into a decision mode.

Anti-pattern 2: Surprise veto

Surprise veto is when someone with authority blocks a decision late – often in a review, a random chat message, or a stakeholder meeting – after weeks of work have already been built on assumptions.

In Helix, design and tech do a two-week implementation spike on stamina. It's not fully committed, but it's "moving." Then the direction owner sees it in a build review and says: "This isn't our game. No."

Design feels betrayed. Tech feels like they wasted time. Producer scrambles to re-plan. The room gets tense, and people start protecting themselves by seeking private approval next time. That creates shadow decisions.

Why it's toxic

Surprise veto punishes initiative and teaches the team that nothing is safe until the last moment. That increases stress because everyone starts working defensively: "Don't commit, don't integrate, don't own."

It also destroys planning credibility. If veto can happen at any time without process, the backlog becomes fiction.

How to recognize it

When people say "we got blindsided" or "we didn't know that was still open," you have surprise veto. The issue is almost never the veto itself. It's the missing commit signal and missing visibility earlier.

Counter: define commit signals and escalation thresholds

You don't eliminate veto power. You eliminate late, invisible veto.

The antidote is:

- Decisions that change scope/pillars/quality must be either explicitly committed or explicitly labeled as exploration.
- Exploration must have a timebox and a decision date.
- If direction owner is the decider, they must be involved at the moment of commitment, not only at the moment of review.
- If something is blocked or contentious, escalate early with a decision-ready package instead of letting it "run" informally.

This ties directly to your escalation topic: escalate deadlocks and risky scope attempts before weeks of execution accumulate.

Also, the decision log helps here: it prevents "I thought it was decided" because the record shows whether it was committed or still open.

Anti-pattern 3: "No one decides, but everyone has an opinion"

This is the most corrosive pattern because it feels like "creative culture" while acting like sabotage.

Nobody owns the call. Everyone feels entitled to weigh in. Feedback arrives from all directions, often late, often contradictory, and often without trade-offs.

In Helix, stamina isn't the only topic. UI tweaks, animation polish, performance budgets, encounter pacing – everyone has opinions. Slack threads run for days. People keep posting references and taste arguments. The producer tries to summarize, but nobody treats the summary as binding because nobody is the decider.

The result is paralysis punctuated by bursts of chaotic action. The project becomes reactive.

Why it's toxic

Opinions are cheap. Implementation is expensive. When the system rewards opinions without requiring responsibility, you get high noise, low progress, and continuous stress.

People also stop trusting each other. Contributors feel ignored. Deciders feel attacked. Producers feel like they're herding cats. Everyone is tired.

How to recognize it

If decisions depend on who spoke last, who posted the best argument, or who escalated to the highest authority, you have this anti-pattern.

If you can't point to a clear decider for recurring decisions, you have this anti-pattern.

Counter: enforce decision rights and shrink the contributor set

You already defined roles: decider / recommender / contributor / informed. This is exactly why they exist.

The antidote is:

- One decider per decision category.

- Contributors limited to people who materially affect constraints and implementation.
- Everyone else is "informed," not "involved."
- Producers enforce that feedback without trade-offs does not change the plan.

This is not about silencing people. It's about making sure input is proportional to consequence.

Why these anti-patterns cluster together

They reinforce each other.

Consensus theater avoids conflict, which delays real decisions.
Delayed decisions create ambiguous commitments.
Ambiguous commitments invite surprise veto.
Surprise veto teaches people to lobby privately.
Private lobbying creates "everyone has an opinion" chaos.
Chaos drives more consensus theater because people become conflict-averse.

It's a loop. If you don't break it, you end up with a team that appears collaborative but feels constantly stressed and ineffective.

Practical counter-measures you can adopt without bureaucracy

You said you want proposals, not just diagnosis. Here's what actually works, in a minimal way.

First, every decision meeting starts with: decision question + decider + timebox + expected output. That kills consensus theater.

Second, every "exploration" gets a label and a stop date: "This is not committed; decision on Friday; if no decision, escalate." That kills surprise veto by forcing earlier visibility and a commit signal.

Third, any scope/pillar/quality change requires the Decision Contract inputs and a decision log entry. Not because you love logging, but because it creates a single reality.

Fourth, producers enforce the "YES gate": no trade-off, no plan change. This reduces opinion-driven creep because it forces people to pay for change.

Fifth, when stuck, escalate as a project risk, not as a personal conflict: option A vs B, costs/risks, pillar impact, what we cut. That prevents politics and keeps authority use clean.

None of this requires corporate process. It requires the courage to be explicit.

The real point

These anti-patterns don't exist because teams are stupid. They exist because teams are trying to be nice under uncertainty.

But nice is not the same as clear.

If you want a calmer production, you don't need fewer hard choices. You need fewer ambiguous non-choices. And you get that by making decision-making explicit, owned, recorded, and translated into backlog reality.

CHAPTER 4:
Change Control (No Bureaucracy)
(evaluate -> decide -> communicate)

I. The difference between a "change" and a "clarification" (not everything needs process)

Most teams suffer from both extremes:

One extreme is **process inflation**: every tiny adjustment becomes a "change request," a meeting, a log entry, a ritual. People stop improving the game because "it's too heavy."

The other extreme is **process starvation**: real scope and direction changes slide in as "quick tweaks," nobody prices the cost, and you wake up a month later with a different game and a broken plan.

The fix is not "more process" or "less process." The fix is being able to tell, quickly and consistently, whether something is a *change* or a *clarification* – and applying the right level of friction.

In a 30–100 person team, this distinction matters because coordination cost is real. If you treat clarifications like changes, you slow down. If you treat changes like clarifications, you create chaos.

Definitions that work in production

A **clarification** is when you make the existing intent more explicit without altering the underlying commitments.

It reduces ambiguity. It does not create new work beyond communication and minor alignment edits. It makes the team more likely to build the same thing.

A **change** is when you alter commitments: scope, pillars, constraints, quality bar, milestone expectations, or the backlog's shape in a way that creates new work, new risk, or new trade-offs.

It may be a good change. But it must be priced and paid for.

The easiest way to remember it:

Clarification reduces interpretation space.
Change alters the plan's physics.

Why teams confuse them (and why it hurts)

Teams label things "clarification" to avoid friction. It's a social move: "I'm not changing anything, I'm just making it clearer." Sometimes it's true. Often it's not.

And teams label things "change" when they're scared of responsibility: "We can't touch anything without a process," which becomes a way to avoid making small improvements and to hide behind procedure.

Both lead to stress:

- If everything is a change, people feel trapped and stop iterating.
- If nothing is a change, planning becomes fiction and work becomes rework.

So you need a simple, shared test.

A practical rule set (adapt it to your system)

Here's a lightweight decision rule that works well as a starting point. Treat it as a template, not a law. The point is to make the classification predictable.

Something is a **clarification** if all of the following are true:

- It does not add new backlog items (or it adds only trivial admin/label updates).
- It does not increase QA surface or integration complexity in a meaningful way.
- It does not change what "done" means for the current milestone/phase.
- It does not force any team to rework already-finished work.

- It does not change pillars, constraints, nongoals, or the phase win condition.

If any of those are false, treat it as a **change.**

Notice what this rule does: it forces you to look at consequences, not wording.

This also helps you avoid the classic trap: “We’re just clarifying,” while quietly moving the goalposts.

Example 1: Clarifying a pillar (wording) vs changing a pillar (priority)

Pillars are a perfect place to get this wrong because the difference can be subtle.

A **pillar clarification** might be:

“We say ‘readability under stress.’ Clarification: this means UI and combat feedback must remain legible at peak intensity, even if we reduce VFX density.”

If the team already agreed that readability wins, and you are simply making the practical interpretation explicit, this is a clarification. The goal didn’t change; you reduced ambiguity. The process can be light: update the one-pager wording, inform leads, done.

A **pillar change** might be:

“We used to prioritize readability over spectacle. Now we want spectacle to win, even if it reduces readability.”

That’s not clarifying. That’s changing what wins. It will affect art direction, effects budgets, UI decisions, performance budgets, and likely scope. This needs the real process: Decision Contract-level decision, decision log entry, one-pager update, and backlog impact.

The test is simple: did the team’s trade-off behavior change? If yes, it’s a change.

Example 2: Tutorial “clarification” vs tutorial change

Tutorials are where teams often hide scope changes inside “clarity.”

A **tutorial clarification** might be:

"We meant the first tutorial prompt to appear after the player performs action X, not immediately on spawn."

If this is a small timing/text adjustment with minimal implementation risk, no new design work, no rework, and no meaningful QA surface increase, it's a clarification. Handle it as a normal backlog tweak: update the ticket, inform the relevant owner, move on.

A **tutorial change** might be:

"We're restructuring the tutorial from 'learn by doing' into a guided step-by-step sequence with additional UI overlays and gating."

That is a real change. It affects design, UX/UI, implementation, localization, QA, and pacing. It also affects your first-hour metrics and possibly your core pillar priorities. This needs pricing and trade-offs.

The key is not whether it's "just tutorial." The key is whether it changes cost, risk, or commitment.

Matching the process to the classification (light vs heavy)

You said your process depends on situation, which is correct. What matters is consistent friction scaling.

A reasonable baseline in a 30–100 team:

For **clarifications**, keep it light:

- Update the one-pager if it's a frame clarification.
- Update the relevant ticket/acceptance criteria if it's execution-level.
- Broadcast the clarification to the impacted leads (short, factual).
- No decision log entry unless you know it will be questioned later.

For **changes**, use your established decision system:

- Required inputs (options, costs, risks, pillar/constraint impact, what gets cut).
- Decider and decision rights are explicit.
- Decision Contract (for scope/pillars/quality-class changes).
- Decision log entry.
- Backlog updated immediately to reflect the new reality.

This avoids both extremes: you don't bureaucratize small clarifications, and you don't allow real changes to sneak in as "clarity."

The two anti-patterns, explicitly

You said both extremes hurt you. Good – because this section is basically about resisting both.

Anti-pattern A: process for everything

The team starts asking permission to clarify obvious intent. That kills iteration speed and creates learned helplessness. People stop improving because "it's not worth the overhead."

Your counter is to legitimize clarifications as low-friction actions, as long as they don't alter commitments.

Anti-pattern B: no process for anything

The team calls real changes "clarifications" to avoid paying trade-offs. That destroys planning. It also creates quiet resentment because people feel tricked into rework.

Your counter is to make the classification test explicit and to treat misclassification as a system failure, not a moral failure. "This turned out to be a change; we need to price it properly."

A producer's closing habit: force the "impact question"

If you want one practical habit that keeps this healthy, it's this:

Whenever someone says "it's just a clarification," ask:
"What changes in the backlog, QA surface, or our pillars/constraints?"

If the answer is "nothing," treat it as a clarification and move fast.
If the answer includes new work, risk, or trade-offs, treat it as a change and route it through the right gate.

That single question prevents both process inflation and process starvation – because it grounds the classification in consequences, not intention.

II. Minimal change pipeline: Evaluate -> Decide -> Communicate

If you want to ship without drowning in scope creep, you need one consistent habit: **changes that affect scope, pillars, or quality must go through a minimal pipeline.**

Not because we love process. Because your biggest problems – no trade-off, backlog chaos, and decisions made in DMs – are all symptoms of the same thing: changes entering the plan without being priced, owned, and made visible.

This pipeline is intentionally small. It doesn't require new meetings. It's designed to fit inside your existing cadence.

And it does **not** apply to everything. If something is a clarification (from the previous topic), keep it light. This pipeline is for real changes – ones that alter commitments.

Why this pipeline works

A change pipeline prevents three predictable failure modes:

No trade-off becomes impossible because evaluation requires pricing and cutting.
Backlog chaos drops because decisions translate into a concrete backlog update, not just talk.
DM decisions stop mattering because a change isn't real until it passes through the pipeline and becomes visible.

The pipeline also reduces stress because it makes change predictable. People stop guessing which random request will suddenly become mandatory. They know there's a gate.

Step 1: Evaluate (price the change before you argue about it)

Evaluation is where most teams lie to themselves. They discuss whether the change is "good" without pricing what it costs and what it displaces.

Minimal evaluation means five things are present, even if rough:

Options (including baseline: "do nothing / not this milestone").
Costs (time, integration, QA surface, opportunity cost).
Risks (failure modes + early signals).
Impact on pillars/constraints (does it strengthen or contradict the frame?).
Trade-off candidate (what gets cut/delayed if accepted).

This doesn't need perfect numbers. It needs honest shape. If the change cannot be priced even roughly, that's already a signal: it's probably too big, too undefined, or too risky to accept casually.

Producer's role in Evaluate: enforce the standard and stop unpriced changes from entering planning. Producers don't need to know every technical detail, but they must know whether the input is decision-ready and who should provide what's missing.

A practical rule you can adopt: if someone brings a change without a trade-off, it's not a change request. It's an idea. Ideas are welcome, but they don't enter the plan for free.

Step 2: Decide (make the call explicit, owned, and backlog-linked)

Decision is the moment the change becomes real – or gets rejected safely.

Two things matter here: **decision rights** and **commit signal**.

Decision rights: the decider depends on change type. That's normal in a domain-decider model. A scope packaging decision might sit with the producer and direction owner. A quality bar decision may require direction owner alignment plus domain constraints (tech/art/QA). A pillar-level change is direction-owner territory.

What matters is not who it is. What matters is that everyone knows who it is before the decision happens.

Commit signal: the decision is not real until it is captured and translated. For these change classes (scope/pillars/quality), that typically means:

- Decision Contract-level capture (minimal fields, not paperwork),
- decision log entry (so it can't become "I didn't know" later),
- backlog update (so execution reality changes).

This is also where you kill DM decisions. A DM can propose. A DM can influence. But it does not commit. The commit happens through the pipeline.

Producer's role in Decide: run the decision mode, keep it timeboxed, and insist that "YES requires a trade-off." This is where your "who can say NO vs who can say YES" rule becomes operational: NO stops intake until trade-off is explicit; YES is granted only through a visible, priced commitment.

If the team cannot decide because it's blocked, this is where escalation fits cleanly: the producer escalates a decision-ready package, not a complaint.

Step 3: Communicate (targeted, fast, and tied to consequences)

Most teams under-communicate changes, then wonder why alignment collapses.

Communication doesn't mean spamming everyone. You chose impacted-only, which is good for 30–100. But "impacted" must be defined by consequences, not by org chart.

If someone's work changes, they are impacted. If someone's dependencies change, they are impacted. If the definition of done changes for their deliverable, they are impacted.

Minimal change communication should always include three elements:

What changed (one sentence).
Why (one sentence: trigger/evidence).
What it means for you (the consequence: what to stop/start/adjust, with link to the backlog/log if relevant).

That's it. Not a novel. Just enough to prevent surprises and shadow work.

Producer's role in Communicate: ensure the message is sent, ensure it's consistent with the decision log and backlog, and ensure it reaches the people who will otherwise find out the hard way.

This step is also where you protect trust. People tolerate hard trade-offs. They don't tolerate being blindsided.

How this stays minimal (and doesn't turn into bureaucracy)

The pipeline is minimal because:

- Evaluate can be a short structured note in a ticket or doc.
- Decide can happen inside an existing lead sync, as long as you enter with a decision-ready package.
- Communicate can be a short targeted message, not a meeting.

The overhead is small compared to the cost of rework from unpriced changes.

A good internal mantra for producers: **small friction early prevents big friction late.**

The "hard line" that makes it work

Here's the one rule that makes the whole pipeline real:

If a change impacts scope, pillars, or quality, and it didn't go through Evaluate -> Decide -> Communicate, then it is not accepted into the plan.

Not because you want control. Because without this line, the pipeline becomes optional – and optional pipelines don't protect scope. They just create extra work for the people who follow them.

Where teams usually break this pipeline (and how to hold it)

You named three pain points. Here's how the pipeline directly counters each:

No trade-off

Evaluate requires trade-off candidates. Decide requires a cut/delay for any YES. If the cut is missing, it's not approved.

Backlog chaos

Decide requires backlog translation. If the backlog doesn't change, the decision didn't happen. This keeps reality in one place.

DM decisions

DMs can't complete the pipeline. They can't be the commit signal. The producer enforces: "Cool idea – route it through evaluation with trade-offs."

This isn't about policing communication. It's about protecting the project from invisible commitments.

What "good" looks like

When this is working, changes still happen – but they feel different:
They are priced before they are adopted.
They have an owner and a date.
They create visible backlog movement.
They are communicated to impacted people fast.
They don't spawn weeks of confusion.

That's the whole point: a minimal pipeline that makes change survivable, without slowing down healthy iteration.

III. Change evaluation: impact on scope, time, cost, risk, quality, pillars

Most teams evaluate changes with vibes.

Someone proposes a change, people react, the loudest concern wins, and the project absorbs the cost later. That's how "small changes" become schedule slips, quality drops, and stress.

A producer-friendly way to fix this is not a heavy scoring system. It's a consistent, lightweight evaluation that forces you to look at the same six dimensions every time:

scope, time, cost, risk, quality, pillars.

This is the heart of the "required decision inputs" topic from Chapter 3. Evaluation is just those inputs focused on one question: what will this change do to the project's reality?

Why a qualitative "traffic light + thresholds" approach fits better than scoring

This part fits the tone presented in my Workbook and is showing that standard. The pattern you've been using is: clear rules, practical thresholds, minimal overhead. A numeric scorecard sounds precise but often becomes fake precision.

So the healthier default is qualitative: **Green / Yellow / Red** per dimension, with a few concrete thresholds that your team can adapt. That keeps it usable across different studio cultures and project types.

The point is not to "compute" a decision. The point is to make trade-offs visible and comparable.

The producer's baseline: evaluation is not debate, it's framing

Evaluation happens *before* the decision meeting turns into discussion.

The producer's job is to ensure the change is framed in a way the decider can safely decide:

- what is being changed,
- what it costs,
- what it risks,
- what it forces you to give up,
- and whether it supports or violates pillars/constraints.

If you skip evaluation, you'll argue in circles: design argues fun, tech argues feasibility, art argues time, QA argues stability. Nobody is wrong, but nobody can decide because the trade-off isn't priced.

Evaluation is how you price it.

The six dimensions (and what "good evaluation" means for each)

1) Scope impact: what expands, what multiplies, what must be cut

Scope is not just "one more feature." It's blast radius: new tasks, new dependencies, new edge cases, new QA surface, new content requirements.

A useful way to evaluate scope is to ask:

- Does this add a new system, or change an existing one?
- Does it create new content obligations (tutorialization, UI, audio, localization)?
- Does it increase permutations (modes, platforms, player states)?

Green scope impact means it's contained, mostly within an existing area, and doesn't multiply permutations.
Red scope impact means it introduces a new surface area or multiplies states.

If scope is Yellow/Red, evaluation must include **what gets cut or deferred**. Without that, you're not evaluating a change – you're accepting scope creep.

2) Time impact: schedule pressure, not just "how many days"

Time is where teams lie. They talk about implementation time and ignore integration time, review time, and "time to discover you were wrong."

The question isn't "how long does it take to code." The question is:

- When does this land in a build?
- How many iterations will it require before it's acceptable?
- Does it steal time from the current phase win condition?

Green time impact means it fits inside existing slack or replaces other work cleanly.
Red time impact means it pushes milestone commitments or delays critical validation.

Your emphasis is "średnio" on runway, but time still matters because time drives burn and morale. Time slip is cost slip.

3) Cost impact: real cost, including opportunity cost

In most teams, "cost" is handwaved because it feels like finance. Don't overcomplicate it. Cost can be expressed as:

- people-weeks,
- contractor needs,
- tooling needs,
- outsourcing implications,
- or simply "this steals X capacity from Y."

Green cost impact means it's absorbed by existing capacity without increasing burn or forcing hidden overtime.
Red cost impact means you're paying with additional headcount, external spend, or sustained overtime.

A common hidden cost: "we can do it" translates to "we will do it at night." That's not free. That's debt with interest.

4) Risk impact: what can fail, and how you'll know early

Risk is not "this feels risky." Risk is a specific failure mode.

Evaluation should name:

- the likely failure mode,
- the consequence if it happens,
- and the earliest signal that tells you it's happening.

Green risk impact means known tech and known pipeline, with early signals and easy rollback.

Red risk impact means unknowns, deep dependencies, or late-stage changes with poor reversibility.

Risk is tightly coupled with scope and time. Bigger scope creates more QA surface, which creates more risk, which degrades quality. If you don't acknowledge that chain, you'll be surprised later.

5) Quality impact: definition-of-done, stability, and the quality bar

Quality impact is often treated as aesthetic. It's broader than that.

Evaluation should ask:

- Does this raise the quality bar (harder to ship), or lower it (debt)?
- Does it affect stability/build health?
- Does it change what "done" means for the milestone?

Green quality impact means it improves quality without creating unstable debt.
Red quality impact means it introduces debt that will be painful to pay, or it risks stability in a phase where stability is the priority.

A classic trick is calling quality erosion "temporary." If it's not explicitly logged and scheduled, it's not temporary – it's permanent.

6) Pillar impact: does it serve what wins, or is it a distraction?

This is the alignment dimension, and it's the one that often saves you from smart-sounding scope creep.

Evaluation must answer:

- Which pillar does this serve, specifically?
- Does it strengthen the current phase win condition?
- Does it conflict with any constraints?

Green pillar impact means it clearly supports a pillar and reinforces current priorities.
Red pillar impact means it's "nice to have," or it optimizes a local preference at the cost of the game's core.

If you cannot connect a change to pillars, it's either premature or misaligned. That doesn't automatically mean "reject," but it should push you toward defer or spike rather than commit.

Two running examples (simple but realistic)

Example A: Tutorial change request

Someone proposes: "Let's add a guided overlay and gating in the first five minutes."

Scope: could be Yellow – new UI states, triggers, localization, edge cases.
Time: Yellow – tutorial work often iterates more than expected.
Cost: Yellow – cross-discipline effort.
Risk: Yellow/Red if late-stage; tutorial changes can create regressions.
Quality: Green if it improves onboarding, Red if it destabilizes build.
Pillars: Green if readability/approachability is a pillar, otherwise Yellow.

A reasonable recommendation might be: **Spike or accept with strict cap**, depending on phase. If you're early and onboarding is critical, accept but pay with an explicit cut elsewhere. If you're late and stability matters, spike in isolation or defer.

Example B: Pillar "clarification" that smells like a pillar change

Someone says: "We're clarifying the pillar 'deep mastery.' We should add a stamina system."

Evaluation quickly reveals whether this is actually a change:

- Pillar impact might be Green, but scope/time/risk could be Red.
- If it forces new systems and new balance work, it's not a clarification – it's a pillar-driven scope change.

A reasonable recommendation might be: **Defer or reject for current milestone**, and log it as a candidate for a later phase, unless you can cut other work to pay for it.

This is why pillars can't be used as laundering. Pillars justify trade-offs; they don't erase costs.

Turning evaluation into a recommendation (accept / reject / defer / spike)

Evaluation is only useful if it leads to a clear action recommendation. Here's a simple decision logic you can adopt and adapt:

Accept when pillar impact is Green and the combined scope/time/risk is manageable *with a stated trade-off*.

Reject when pillar impact is Yellow/Red and scope/time/risk is high, or when the change violates a nongoal/constraint.

Defer when the change is valuable but doesn't fit current phase priorities or would destabilize the milestone.

Spike when the value is plausible but uncertainty is high – meaning you need evidence before committing.

What matters: every "accept" must name what you cut or delay. Otherwise you're not accepting a change – you're accepting entropy.

The producer's closing move: capture the evaluation in a reusable form

You don't need a heavy template here, but you do need consistency.

A good habit is to capture the evaluation in the same place the change request lives (ticket/doc), in a small structured block:

- brief summary,
- the six dimensions as Green/Yellow/Red with one sentence each,
- recommended action (accept/reject/defer/spike),
- and if accept: the trade-off and the owner/next step.

Then, if it becomes a real scope/pillar/quality change, it flows into the Decision Contract and decision log. That's how your system stays coherent: evaluation feeds decision, decision feeds backlog, backlog feeds reality.

The end result is not "less change." It's **less chaos per change** – because every meaningful change is priced, aligned, and paid for.

IV. Change categories (e.g., must-fix / compliance / polish / nice-to-have) and what each implies

Change categories are not about labels. They're about **what a change is allowed to do to your plan.**

In mid-production you're constantly balancing two truths:

- The game needs iteration to get better.
- The project needs stability to ship.

If you treat every change as "important," you get chaos. If you treat every change as "disruptive," you freeze and ship something mediocre.

So you need a small set of categories that turn emotional debates into predictable decisions. Categories don't replace evaluation (scope/time/risk/quality/pillars). They **pre-frame** it: they tell you what you're optimizing for when this change enters the pipeline.

A useful classification in the workbook spirit should be language-based and practical. No corporate numbering. Just categories that imply consequences.

Must-fix: "we can't ship like this"

This category exists to protect the integrity of the product and the team. It should be rare, and it must be respected.

A must-fix implies that the current state is unacceptable for shipping because it breaks the core promise of the game or creates severe harm. This includes the obvious: crashes, data loss, broken saves, hard blockers. But in practice, in mid-production, it can also include "core loop is broken" or "tutorial fails in a way that stops players from understanding the game," because those are effectively product-stoppers even if they're not technical crashes.

The implication is simple: **must-fix work is allowed to displace other work.** Not for free, but with an explicit trade-off. If a must-fix appears, something else must move. If you pretend you'll "just squeeze it in," you're lying to your schedule and your team.

The must-fix trap is overuse. Teams sometimes label uncomfortable problems as must-fix to force priority. That destroys trust. A healthy rule is: must-fix is for "stop-ship" class outcomes, not for "this bothers me."

Compliance: "external rules that don't care about your vision"

Compliance changes are special because they are not negotiated by taste. They are negotiated by external constraints.

In games, "compliance" often means platform requirements and certification realities (especially on consoles), but it's broader than that: privacy and data handling, age ratings, UGC moderation obligations, licensing constraints, trademark issues, accessibility requirements in certain contexts, store policy rules, and even region-specific legal constraints depending on features.

The key implication: **compliance work is deadline-shaped.** You don't "get to it when you feel like it." If compliance is discovered late, it becomes a schedule bomb and forces low-quality rushed implementations.

So the practical mid-production rule is: treat compliance as a pipeline with early discovery. When a compliance issue appears, you evaluate it like any change (scope/time/risk), but you also add one extra reality: external deadlines and rejection risk. That often makes compliance closer to must-fix in its displacement power.

The compliance trap is denial. Teams avoid it because it feels unfun. Then it lands late, and suddenly you're paying with crunch and sloppy solutions.

Polish: "raising perceived quality without changing the product"

Polish is the most dangerous category because it can be either healthy refinement or slow-motion scope creep, depending on how you define it.

In a clean definition, polish improves presentation, clarity, and feel **without adding new feature surface.** It sharpens what already exists: readability, feedback, pacing, UX friction, animation timing, audio mix, VFX density, copy, tutorial clarity, small tuning passes.

The implication you want in mid-production is: **polish is allowed as a steady stream, but it must be capped and timeboxed.**

If you treat polish as "only at the end," you often arrive at the end with a mountain of papercuts and no time to fix them. If you treat polish as unlimited, it becomes an excuse to endlessly re-touch everything and destabilize scope.

So the healthy stance is conditional: polish can run continuously, but the project must have circumstances that justify how much polish is allowed at a given moment. If build stability is collapsing, polish shrinks. If you're validating the first hour, polish grows there and shrinks elsewhere. If you're approaching milestone commitments, polish becomes more selective and more constrained.

The polish trap is mislabeling. "Just polish" sometimes hides new UI states, new tutorial gating, new content requirements, or new mechanics changes. That's not polish. That's change. Categories exist to prevent this kind of laundering.

Nice-to-have: "valuable, but not required to win"

Nice-to-have is where scope creep lives when it's trying to sound reasonable.

A nice-to-have change might genuinely improve the game. But it's not required to meet the current phase win condition or to ship a coherent product. The key implication: **nice-to-have is always pay-to-play.**

Meaning: it must come with an explicit trade-off and it must survive evaluation against pillars and constraints. If it can't name what it replaces, it doesn't enter the plan. It goes into a parking lot or a future bucket.

Nice-to-have also implies a different default action: defer is often the correct answer unless you have slack or you can replace lower-value work.

The nice-to-have trap is "death by a thousand upgrades." Each request is small and sounds harmless. Together, they erase your schedule.

What categories imply in the change pipeline

These categories become useful only when they change behavior in Evaluate -> Decide -> Communicate.

In evaluation, categories tell you what to look for:

- Must-fix: identify stop-ship criteria, root cause, and fastest safe fix; avoid “perfect fix” fantasies.
- Compliance: identify deadline and rejection risk; prefer earlier integration to avoid late surprises.
- Polish: confirm it doesn’t add scope; demand tight caps and clear success criteria.
- Nice-to-have: demand trade-offs and alignment; default to defer.

In decision-making, categories define how much displacement power the change has:

- Must-fix and compliance can legitimately displace other work, but still require explicit trade-offs so the plan stays honest.
- Polish can displace only within its allocated budget/timebox unless the team explicitly reclassifies it.
- Nice-to-have cannot displace anything unless something else is cut.

In communication, categories control how you message changes:

- Must-fix and compliance should be communicated fast to impacted people because they reshape priorities and often affect multiple domains.
- Polish changes should be communicated when they affect coordination (e.g., altered acceptance criteria), not as noise.
- Nice-to-have should be communicated as “accepted with trade-off” or “captured/deferred,” to prevent silent expectation buildup.

A practical warning: categories are not a substitute for trade-offs

Teams often use categories as a way to avoid thinking: “It’s must-fix, so we do it.” That’s how you get runaway. Even must-fix work must be paid for, because time is finite.

Categories should shorten the argument, not end it:

- They tell you what the default should be.
- They don't erase the need for explicit trade-offs.

The outcome you're aiming for

When categories are working, the team stops fighting about whether a change is "good." They start asking better questions:

Is this stop-ship, compliance, polish, or nice-to-have?
What does that imply about displacement and trade-offs?
Does it support pillars and the current phase win condition?
What do we cut or defer to pay for it?

That's how you keep mid-production adaptive without turning it into entropy.

V. When a change is automatically "risk": thresholds (e.g., touches core loop, saves, perf, platform)

Some changes are risky not because your team is careless, but because the surface they touch is fragile.

You can argue about risk all day, but in practice you need a shortcut: **a set of thresholds where a change is automatically classified as "risk"** – meaning it must trigger extra rigor in evaluation, decision, and verification.

This is not paranoia. It's how you protect shipping reality. Especially in mid-production, where you still need iteration, but you can't afford hidden landmines. And it becomes even more important in late production / pre-cert, where reversibility drops and the cost of regressions explodes.

The guiding scenario: "we'll just tweak stamina"

You're mid-production. The game has a working loop. Someone proposes a stamina tweak: small numbers, "just tuning." It sounds safe.

But the tweak touches the core loop: movement, attack cadence, regen pacing. It also affects tutorial messaging and AI behavior (because enemy timing assumes certain player capacity). Suddenly you're not tuning a number. You're changing the game's physics.

This is exactly why thresholds matter. Without them, teams under-react to high-risk surfaces because the change looks small.

What "auto-risk" means operationally

When a change crosses an auto-risk threshold, you don't automatically reject it. You automatically change *how you treat it*.

Auto-risk implies:

- you must run the full change evaluation lens (scope/time/cost/risk/ quality/pillars) with explicit attention to downstream effects,

- you must have a decider and a visible commit signal (no DM approvals),
- you must plan verification beyond "it seems fine on my machine,"
- and you should have a rollback plan or safe fallback if the change misbehaves.

This ties directly to your minimal pipeline (Evaluate -> Decide -> Communicate), required decision inputs, and decision log. Auto-risk changes are where those tools actually pay for themselves.

Universal auto-risk thresholds (the surfaces you don't "just tweak")

Universal and general thresholds that apply to most game projects regardless of genre or tech stack. Think of these as "if it touches this, treat it as risk."

Core loop interactions

Anything that changes the timing, economy, rules, or feedback of the top 1–3 player actions that define the game. If it affects what the player does every minute, it's high leverage and high regression potential. Your stamina tweak fits here.

Why it's auto-risk: the core loop has the most dependencies – tutorial, AI, difficulty, UX, content pacing, player psychology. Small loop changes produce big ripple effects.

Save/load and persistence

Anything that touches save format, serialization, progression flags, inventory, or the rules that determine what is persisted.

Why it's auto-risk: persistence bugs are catastrophic. They destroy trust instantly, are hard to reproduce, and can brick player progress. Late in production, save changes become especially dangerous because you also introduce migration concerns.

Performance budgets and runtime-critical code paths

Anything that touches your main update loop, rendering, streaming, memory budgets, or frame-time-critical systems.

Why it's auto-risk: performance regressions are often non-linear and content-dependent. You can "test it" in one scene and still ship a regression in another. Performance is also tightly coupled with quality: a performance fix can degrade visuals; a visual "improvement" can tank framerate.

Platform-specific requirements and submission surfaces

Anything that touches platform SDK integrations, input compliance, save handling rules, entitlement checks, TRCs/TCRs/XRs, storefront flows, or any feature that tends to fail certification.

Why it's auto-risk: platform rules are external and unforgiving. Failures cost calendar time, morale, and often force rushed changes late.

Networking / determinism / multiplayer state (if applicable)

Even if your game is mostly single-player, any netcode or synchronized state is fragile.

Why it's auto-risk: the bug surface is multiplied by latency, timing, and state divergence. These changes require verification beyond local testing.

Progression economy and reward loops

XP curves, loot tables, unlock rules, currency sinks – anything that alters the incentive structure.

Why it's auto-risk: economy changes can destabilize player behavior, pacing, and retention. They also create balance debt. In mid-production you can iterate; late production you must be cautious because tuning changes can invalidate content difficulty and QA baselines.

You don't need a longer list. Most "we didn't expect this" disasters come from ignoring one of these surfaces.

Why late production makes these thresholds stricter

In mid-production, you can take some risk if you have time to learn. In late production, the same change becomes more dangerous because:

- the QA surface is bigger,
- the content is closer to final,
- the team is under ship pressure,
- and regressions become harder to isolate.

So the exact same stamina tweak that was “fine” earlier becomes an auto-risk with heavier verification later.

A practical mindset: as you approach pre-cert / release, **your auto-risk list doesn’t change, but your tolerance does**. The gate gets narrower.

What to do when something is auto-risk (the minimal extra rigor)

Add a rule beyond classification. Here’s a minimal set that keeps this sane, not bureaucratic.

If a change is auto-risk, it must include:

- a clear baseline and rollback path (what happens if we revert? what data breaks?),
- a verification plan that matches the surface (for saves: load old saves; for perf: test representative content; for platform: test submission-critical flows),
- and an explicit trade-off if it displaces other work.

This does not require huge docs. It requires explicitness.

In practice, it means you don’t accept “it’s a small tweak” as an argument. You accept “it’s a small tweak and here’s how we’ll detect regressions quickly.”

How this integrates into your existing decision system

Auto-risk is not a separate process. It is a trigger that forces your existing process to be used properly.

Change evaluation: auto-risk should immediately flag higher risk weight and downstream dependencies.
Decision meetings: auto-risk changes require pre-read; you don’t discover risk in the meeting.
Decision log: auto-risk decisions should be logged because they’re likely to be questioned later, and because they often explain why a milestone shifted.
Communication: impacted people must be informed early because auto-risk changes affect multiple domains even when they look local.

This is also how you reduce DM decisions. Auto-risk surfaces are exactly where informal approvals do the most damage.

The producer's closing habit: "surface check" before you discuss the idea

If you want one simple habit: when a change is proposed, ask one question first:

"What surface does this touch?"

If the answer is core loop, saves, perf, or platform, you don't debate taste yet. You mark it auto-risk and route it through the stricter gate: explicit evaluation, explicit decision, explicit verification.

That's how you keep iteration alive without letting the project become a minefield.

VI. Communicating the decision: who must know, in what order, how to avoid rumors

A change decision isn't real when it's "decided." It's real when the right people update their behavior.

That only happens when communication is fast, consistent, and tied to concrete consequences (backlog, acceptance criteria, priorities). If you don't do this, the team will fill the vacuum with guesses. And guesses become rumors.

In mid-sized teams (30–100), rumors rarely come from malice. They come from two things you named: **no updates** and **"someone said something"**. A half-heard sentence from a meeting becomes truth because there's no authoritative, visible source to contradict it.

So the goal of change communication is not "broadcast information." The goal is to create a single, durable reality that beats hallway conversations.

Who must know (define "impacted" by behavior change)

The clean rule is: **impacted means the decision changes what someone will do, stop doing, or how their work will be evaluated.**

That typically includes:

- anyone whose current tasks must change (start/stop/redo),
- anyone who owns dependencies or integrations affected by the change,
- anyone whose acceptance criteria or definition-of-done shifts,
- anyone who will receive questions from others because they are the local "authority" (leads).

Avoid the two extremes:

- informing everyone about everything (noise -> people tune out),
- informing only a tiny circle (vacuum -> rumors).

Targeted communication works when “impacted” is precise and when there’s a stable place to point people to.

In what order (principles, not a rigid chain)

Use principles rather than a strict sequence. Here are the ones that keep teams calm.

Principle 1: Align the people who will be asked first.

Before you announce broadly, make sure the leads who will receive questions have the same message. If leads interpret the change differently, you don’t have rumors – you have parallel realities.

This doesn’t mean a new meeting. It can be a quick pre-brief in the same channel: “Here is the decision, here is what changes, here is what doesn’t.”

Principle 2: Update reality before you narrate reality.

If the backlog and source-of-truth documents are not updated, your message is just words. Words lose to tickets.

So the correct order is usually:

1. update the backlog / acceptance criteria / milestone board,
2. log the decision (if it’s scope/pillar/quality class),
3. then communicate the change with links.

This single habit kills the “no updates” rumor engine.

Principle 3: Communicate proportional to impact and reversibility.

Small changes can be communicated in a short note to impacted people. High-impact or hard-to-reverse changes deserve a slightly more formal note and a clearer “why,” because people will otherwise invent motives.

Principle 4: Give people the "what does this mean for me" hook.

Most rumor cycles start because people don't know how the change affects their work today. If you don't tell them, they will ask each other and amplify partial answers.

So every message must answer: what changes, what doesn't, what you should do now.

How to avoid rumors (kill the two root causes)

You identified them. Let's tackle them directly.

Rumor source #1: "No updates"

When backlog and docs don't change, the team assumes the decision is either fake, political, or unstable. People keep working on the old plan "just in case," which creates divergence and rework.

Counter: treat backlog/doc updates as part of the decision itself. If updates aren't made, the decision didn't happen. This is a producer discipline.

Rumor source #2: "Someone said something"

This happens when decisions are discussed in meetings, but the outcome is not captured in a clear, single statement that everyone can reference. People quote fragments: "I think we cut X?" "I heard we're changing the pillar?" That becomes social truth.

Counter: one canonical message, with one canonical record. If people ask, you point to the same place every time. The fastest rumor-killer is consistency.

Also: explicitly mark what is *not decided*. Uncertainty is fine. Hidden uncertainty is what breeds rumors.

The producer's job: create an authoritative trail, not more chatter

Since you're writing this series in a producer-forward voice, it's worth stating plainly: **the producer owns the coherence of the communication, not necessarily the content of the decision.**

That means:

- ensure the plan reflects the decision,

- ensure the message is unambiguous,
- ensure impacted people see it quickly,
- ensure follow-up questions don't fork the narrative.

If communication is left as an afterthought, the team will produce its own narrative. And it won't be the one you want.

What a good change announcement contains (minimal but complete)

A good message is short, but it includes the pieces that stop speculation.

It should contain:

- a one-sentence decision statement (what),
- one-sentence reason (why now),
- explicit trade-off or consequence (what moved / what got cut),
- "what this means for you" (action),
- link to updated backlog / decision log entry (source of truth),
- and a line stating what is still open, if anything.

The trade-off line is important. Without it, people assume the decision was arbitrary or political, because they can't see the cost being paid.

A copyable template (adapt to your team's channels)

Use this as a default. It's designed to be pasted into whatever durable channel your team uses. Keep it short.

Subject/Title: Change decision: [X] (effective [date])

Message:
We decided to **[do X / stop doing Y / move Z]**.
Why: **[one sentence trigger/evidence]**.
Trade-off: **[what we cut/delayed/deprioritized, or what budget we are spending]**.
Impact: If you're working on **[areas/epics]**, please **[stop/start/adjust]** and follow the updated tickets.
Source of truth: **[link to updated backlog item(s) and/or decision log entry]**.
Still open (if applicable): **[what isn't decided yet + when it will be decided]**.

This template prevents "someone said something" because it creates a stable quote. It prevents "no updates" because it forces you to link to reality.

One last practical tip: don't let follow-ups fork the decision

After a decision is communicated, people will ask clarifying questions. That's normal. The danger is when those questions get answered in private DMs with new commitments.

If a question implies a new commitment or a new trade-off, it's not a clarification – it's a new change. Route it back through the pipeline. Otherwise you rebuild the rumor engine you just tried to shut down.

When communication is done right, the team doesn't feel controlled. They feel safe: the plan is real, changes are visible, and they don't have to guess.

VII. How to say "no" without conflict: ready-made phrasing and "trade" (what we do instead)

Most conflict around "no" isn't about the refusal. It's about the uncertainty it creates.

People can handle "we're not doing this." What they can't handle is "we're not doing this, and I don't know what happens next." That ambiguity turns a reasonable "no" into a power struggle, because the other side has no stable alternative.

You said the main reason for "no" here is **lack of data**. That's one of the healthiest reasons to say no – if you say it properly. The goal is not to shut ideas down. The goal is to stop the team from committing to something unpriced and then paying the cost in rework.

So the shape of a good "no" in this chapter is:

No, not yet – because we don't have the inputs. Here's what we need, who owns it, and what we do until then.

That last part is the "trade." Not always "cut feature X," but always something that ties back to execution: backlog, spike, smaller version, or defer bucket with a decision date.

The producer's stance: "no" is a safety stop, not a verdict

A producer isn't saying "no" to creativity. They're saying "no" to making commitments without evidence.

This is consistent with everything you built so far: required decision inputs, decision meetings, escalation, decision log, and the minimal change pipeline. A "no" that doesn't reference those systems will feel personal. A "no" that does feels procedural and fair.

Also: saying "no" without conflict doesn't mean being soft. It means being **explicit** about the reason, the missing inputs, and the next step.

What "trade" means when the reason is "lack of data"

When you lack data, the trade is usually one of these:

- we do a timeboxed spike instead of committing,
- we ship a smaller version that fits current constraints,
- we defer and set a decision date + success criteria,
- or we accept only if we cut something else to buy time for validation.

The key is that the trade must result in a concrete backlog action. Otherwise you're just negotiating emotions.

Ready-made phrasing (assertive, factual, with a next step)

Below are ~10 templates you can use internally or with external stakeholders. They all share the same structure: stop the commitment, explain why, propose the trade, anchor it to execution.

1. **"Not ready to decide."**
   "We don't have enough data to commit to this. If we want it on the table, we need a quick spike to answer [unknown X]. Until then, it stays out of the committed backlog."

2. **"Show me the trade."**
   "I'm not saying no to the idea. I'm saying no to adding it without a trade-off. What do we cut or move to pay for it? If we can't name that, it's a defer."

3. **"Make it decision-ready."**
   "Right now this is an opinion, not a decision proposal. Bring it back with two options, rough cost/risk, and how it impacts pillars. Then we can decide fast."

4. **"Evidence first, commitment later."**
   "This touches a high-risk surface. I won't approve it based on gut feel. Let's define what evidence we need and run a timeboxed test. If the test passes, we reconsider."

5. **"Defer with a date."**
   "I'm saying 'no for now.' We'll revisit after [milestone/feature freeze/playtest], with a clear decision date. If we don't schedule the revisit, it turns into background pressure and chaos."

6. **"Smaller version, now."**
   "We can't afford the full version. If we want the benefit, we can

do a smaller version that fits the current scope budget: [smaller scope]. Anything bigger needs a cut."

7. **"Clarify the goal."**
   "I'm not confident we're solving the right problem yet. What's the player-facing outcome we're trying to achieve? Once we agree on that, we can pick the cheapest option that gets us there."

8. **"No DM commitments."**
   "Let's not treat this as approved until it's in the backlog with an owner and trade-off. Otherwise we'll create parallel realities and rework."

9. **"This is a spike, not a feature."**
   "We can allocate [X days] to validate feasibility and value. That's a spike with a defined question and exit criteria. It's not an implementation commitment."

10. **"Stop-ship surfaces need proof."**
    "This touches [core loop/saves/perf/platform]. That automatically elevates risk. If we do it, we need a rollback plan and explicit verification steps. If we can't afford that, the answer is no."

These phrases work because they don't attack the person. They attack the missing inputs and the process bypass.

How to "trade" without sounding like a negotiator

A common mistake is presenting trade-offs as personal bargaining: "If you want X, you need to give me Y." That can feel political.

Instead, frame the trade as physics: time and capacity are finite; your plan must stay coherent. The producer is simply making the cost visible.

A clean phrasing pattern is:

"If we do this, we must stop doing something else. Here are the two candidates that are closest in value/cost. Which do we prefer to trade?"

Notice what this does: it moves conflict from "your idea vs my resistance" to "two explicit options with consequences." That's where adults can decide.

A mini playbook for internal vs external "no"

You said both internal and external.

Internally, you can be more direct about process:

- "We don't have the inputs."
- "This isn't in the committed backlog."
- "We need a trade-off."

Externally (publisher/marketing/stakeholder), the same logic applies but you translate jargon into outcomes:

- "We can't commit without validation."
- "We can propose two options with costs and risks by [date]."
- "If we include this, we must remove/shift [something], otherwise the delivery risk increases."

The mistake externally is overpromising while you "buy time." That creates later conflict. A clean no now prevents a bigger no later.

The crucial finishing move: define what happens next

You explicitly said: "trzeba ustalić co się ma wydarzyć." Exactly.

A "no" without next step is just a wall. A "no" with a next step is a gate. So always close with one of these:

- "Spike owner is X, question is Y, timebox is Z, decision date is D."
- "Deferred to post-milestone; captured in backlog bucket; revisit on D."
- "Rejected for this phase because it violates [pillar/constraint]; can be reconsidered only if [condition]."
- "Accepted only if we cut/move [item]; update backlog today."

That's how you say no without conflict: you remove ambiguity, you show the trade, and you keep the project's reality coherent.

VIII. Anti-patterns: "silent changes", "adding it to the board without a decision", "change as a reward for shouting"

These three anti-patterns feel different, but they share one outcome: **the plan stops being believable.**

And once people stop believing the plan, you don't have production anymore. You have improvisation with a schedule attached. That's when stress climbs, accountability gets blurry, and the team starts protecting itself instead of shipping.

Let's try to anchor this mainly in communication - and that's exactly where these patterns breed. When change enters through informal channels, the backlog becomes a rumor tracker, not a control system.

Let's use one guiding story and watch how a team drifts into all three patterns.

The guiding story: the "small UX tweak" that quietly rewrote the milestone

Mid-production, team around 50. The milestone is tight but doable. Everyone is tired but stable.

A designer notices that the onboarding flow is slightly confusing. They write a short message in chat: "We should add one more tutorial prompt here." It gets a few thumbs-up. Someone from UX adds: "Also, can we add a highlight and block input until the player clicks it? Super quick."

No one is being malicious. The intent is good.

But three things happen next:

1. The tweak gets implemented quietly by someone helpful.
2. It isn't evaluated for scope/time/risk.
3. It isn't communicated as a decision with consequences.

Over the next week, three different people touch it, each adding a "small improvement." QA now has new states to test. Localization notices new strings late. Tech sees a minor regression in input flow. And suddenly the milestone feels like it's slipping "for no reason."

This is not because the tweak was wrong. It's because the system allowed change to become real without passing through Evaluate -> Decide -> Communicate.

Now let's map this story to the three anti-patterns.

Anti-pattern 1: Silent changes

A silent change is any change that becomes reality without leaving a visible trail that impacted people can follow.

It often starts in chat. Someone proposes it, someone does it, and everyone assumes "it's fine" because it was small. Then the consequences hit later in a different domain, and nobody can answer: when did we agree to this?

Silent changes are especially toxic because they don't just cause rework. They cause **trust collapse**. The team learns that "the plan is not real," and they adjust their behavior accordingly:

- leads stop committing,
- engineers stop refactoring safely,
- QA stops trusting acceptance criteria,
- producers spend time chasing ghosts.

A silent change also creates blame traps, because once it hurts, people look for someone to blame – when the real cause was process leakage.

Safety mechanism: make "visibility" non-optional for scope/quality/pillar-impacting change.

A minimal rule that works: if a change affects behavior, scope, definition-of-done, or QA surface, it must leave a trace in the durable system (ticket/backlog + short note). If it doesn't, it gets treated as not accepted and may be reverted.

This is not bureaucracy. It's a shared memory.

Anti-pattern 2: Adding it to the board without a decision

This one is subtle because boards feel like "truth." If something is on the board, people assume it was decided.

So a common failure mode is: someone adds a ticket "just to track it," but the board turns it into an implied commitment. Or a lead adds it to a sprint as a "maybe," and it becomes real because people start working.

In the story, someone creates a task: "Improve tutorial flow." It gets placed in the milestone column because it "seems small." No trade-off. No decider. No explicit yes. But now it's in the same visual space as committed milestone work, so it competes for attention and capacity.

This destroys trust because the team can't tell what is committed versus what is aspirational. The board stops representing reality. It represents pressure.

Safety mechanism: separate "captured ideas" from "committed scope."

You don't need a complex system. You need one explicit distinction. For example, a different bucket/status for "candidate changes" that are not approved, or a simple rule: nothing enters the committed milestone lane without an explicit decision and trade-off.

Then enforce it: if something is put into committed lanes without a decision, the producer moves it out immediately. Not as punishment – because otherwise your visual system lies.

This ties directly to your earlier rule: a YES requires a gate. A board placement is not a gate.

Anti-pattern 3: Change as a reward for shouting

This is the cultural rot that emerges when the process is weak.

If the loudest person gets their change accepted, you train the team to shout. Not necessarily literally – sometimes it's persistent pinging, emotional framing, escalating in DMs, or pushing urgency without data.

In the story, one person keeps pushing: "This is important, we'll lose players." They repeat it in multiple channels. People get tired. Eventually someone says yes just to end the noise. Now the team learns a lesson: volume beats evaluation.

Once that happens, quiet, thoughtful people disengage, and your change pipeline becomes a popularity contest. That is the fastest way to lose trust in planning.

Treat this primarily as a process problem. That's correct. When the gate is real, shouting stops working.

Safety mechanism: remove "volume" as an input.

The rule is: changes are decided based on evaluation, not persistence. If someone wants a change, they don't shout. They provide decision-ready inputs: impact on scope/time/risk/quality/pillars and a trade-off. Without that, the request doesn't advance.

A second mechanism: create a predictable cadence for considering non-urgent changes (weekly triage, or a fixed window). That prevents people from trying to "win" by interrupting.

The unifying fix: one allowed path for change to become real

All three anti-patterns are leaks around the same pipe. So the fix is not three separate policies. It's one rule:

For scope/quality/pillar-impacting changes, the only path is: Evaluate -> Decide -> Communicate.

If a change didn't go through that, it is not accepted as plan reality. It may exist as an idea or a candidate. But it doesn't get to consume capacity as if it was approved.

And to protect trust, you also need the practical implementation detail:

- update the backlog as part of the decision,
- communicate to impacted people with a clear "what changed / why / trade-off / what to do now,"
- and log the decision when it's in the "we will argue about this later" category.

That's how you prevent "someone said something" from becoming the de facto process.

Two small thresholds that keep you sane

Minimal rules + thresholds, here are two that work well without creating paperwork:

Threshold A: if it creates new QA surface, it is not silent.

New states, new strings, new edge cases, new platform behaviors – this needs visibility and communication.

Threshold B: if it changes the committed milestone lane, it requires an explicit trade-off.

If something goes in, something comes out or moves. Otherwise you're lying to the plan.

These thresholds directly defend trust. They make the plan stable enough that people can execute without guessing.

Why this matters more than you think

Teams can survive missed estimates. They can survive a few bad calls. What they struggle to survive is a plan that behaves like a rumor.

Silent changes, board-without-decision, and shouting-reward all teach the same lesson: "planning is theater." Once that lesson spreads, you can't fix it with more meetings. You fix it by making the change pipeline real, and by enforcing that reality is created through explicit decisions – not through noise.

CHAPTER 5:
Momentum Principles & Early Signals
(what kills momentum; how to spot it early)

I. Momentum defined: steady "done" flow and predictability

Momentum in game development is not "everyone is busy."

It's not a mood. It's not the number of tasks closed in Jira. It's not how many hours the team put in last week.

Momentum is steady, repeatable flow of real "done" work, and the predictability that comes from it.

If you're a producer or a lead, that definition matters because it separates two very different project states that look similar on the surface:

- A team can look active (lots of tasks moving) while delivering almost nothing integrated and shippable.
- A team can look "slow" (less churn, fewer started tasks) while quietly shipping real increments every week.

The difference is momentum.

A guiding story: the "busy" project that couldn't finish anything

Let's call it Project Drift. Mid-sized team, mixed disciplines, mid-production. Daily standups feel energetic. The board is full. People are working hard.

But the build doesn't improve. Every review is a scramble. Features are "almost done" for weeks. QA keeps finding regressions in areas that were supposedly finished. Leads start adding buffers to every estimate because nothing lands when expected.

The project isn't lacking effort. It's lacking momentum.

Two root causes show up immediately:

1. "Done" is not defined in a way that forces integration and verification.
2. Priorities keep changing, so work keeps getting reopened or rerouted.

Those two killers – vague done and shifting priorities – create the illusion of progress while starving the project of actual delivered value.

What "done" means in a momentum definition (and why it must be strict)

For momentum, "done" needs to mean **integrated, verified, and shippable at the quality bar of the current phase.**

Not "implemented on a branch." Not "works on my machine." Not "design done" in isolation. Those are intermediate states. They can be useful internally, but they don't create momentum. They create inventory.

You can absolutely define stage-specific "done" for sub-work (e.g., "art done" or "design done"), but if you do, you must be honest: that's **done-for-stage**, not done-for-ship. Momentum is measured in done-for-ship increments, because only those reduce uncertainty and build predictability.

The moment you allow "done" to mean "handed off," you convert your schedule into a handoff lottery.

Momentum vs velocity: why velocity lies

Velocity often measures activity inside your process, not delivery to a stable build.

In Project Drift, velocity looks great: many tasks moved to "done" according to local definitions. But the build doesn't get more stable, the milestone doesn't get closer, and QA load doesn't go down. That's because velocity is counting local completion, not integrated completion.

Momentum doesn't care how many points you burned. It cares whether the game is actually getting more complete and more predictable.

A blunt way to say it:

Velocity can be faked by redefining "done." Momentum can't.

Momentum is visible in the build and in the ability to forecast.

Predictability is the product of momentum

Predictability isn't about perfect estimates. It's about having a system that consistently turns work into done.

When you have momentum, you can say things like:

- "We reliably finish 6–8 real items per week at this scope/quality."
- "When we start something, it lands in X days, not 'eventually'."
- "Changes in priority have a visible cost, and we pay it explicitly."

When you don't have momentum, everything becomes negotiation and hope:

- "It's almost done" becomes a permanent status.
- Deadlines become fake.
- Plans become vibes.

As a producer/lead, your goal is not to create a perfect plan. Your goal is to create a project that behaves predictably under imperfect information.

That's momentum.

What kills momentum

Based on two killers: lack of "done" definition and constant priority shifts. These are tightly linked.

No definition of done creates endless partial work. People stop at "my part is done" and push uncertainty downstream. Downstream then pushes back: integration breaks, QA finds issues, design changes, and work reopens. You get churn, not flow.

Priority shifts prevent completion. Work gets started, then paused, then resumed. Context is lost. Dependencies rot. The team carries a growing pile of half-finished inventory, and inventory is poison for predictability.

Combined, these two create a project where nothing truly finishes, so everything remains uncertain, so priorities keep changing "to fix it," which creates even less finishing. It's a loop.

Momentum breaks that loop by making "finish and integrate" the default, and by putting a cost on priority changes.

2–3 simple indicators that reveal momentum (without agile religion)

A few simple indicators. Here are three that work in real studios because they are hard to game and easy to interpret.

1) Throughput of real "done" items

How many items per week actually meet the strict done definition (integrated + verified). Trend matters more than the absolute number.

If throughput is unstable or near zero while the team is "busy," you have a flow problem.

2) Age of work items (time-in-progress)

How long does it take for an item to go from "started" to "done"? When items routinely sit in progress for weeks, you're accumulating uncertainty and rework risk.

A project with momentum has items that move through consistently. A project without momentum has items that stall and resurrect.

3) Reopen / churn rate

How often do "done" items come back? How often does work bounce between states? This is the clean signal for "done definition is fake" and "priorities are thrashing."

If churn is high, predictability is impossible because the system can't keep promises.

You don't need more metrics than this. These three tell you whether your project is delivering reality or just moving cards.

The practical definition you can use with leads

If you want a one-line definition you can repeat in lead sync without sounding like you're importing process culture, use this:

Momentum is a steady stream of integrated, verified "done," plus the ability to predict what will be done next week.

If you can't predict next week, you don't have momentum. You have motion.

What "good momentum" would look like in the guiding story

If Project Drift fixed only two things – strict done and controlled priority changes – the entire feel of production would change.

Strict done would force integration earlier, reduce surprise QA debt, and make the build improve in visible increments. Controlled priority changes would stop the backlog from becoming a rotating door and would allow work to actually land.

Then throughput stabilizes, item age drops, churn drops. Not because people suddenly got better, but because the system stopped rewarding partial completion.

And that's the real producer/lead takeaway:

Momentum is not a motivational speech. It's a structural property of how work finishes.

II. Early signals of momentum loss: growing WIP, falling close rate, no builds, priority conflicts

Momentum usually doesn't die in a dramatic explosion. It dies quietly, one "small exception" at a time.

A team feels busy. Meetings keep happening. People keep committing. And yet the project stops producing real "done" flow. You only realize it's serious when the milestone suddenly becomes impossible and everyone is stressed.

The good news is: momentum loss leaves early signals. They're not subtle. Teams just ignore them because each signal has a convenient excuse.

I'll reuse the same guiding project from the previous topic – Project Drift – because these signals tend to appear together and reinforce each other.

Project Drift: the moment the flow starts to rot

Project Drift is mid-production. The board is full, but "done" is scarce. Builds are unstable. Priorities change weekly. People are working hard, yet the game isn't getting more complete.

Here are the early signals that show momentum is bleeding out – before it becomes a crisis.

Signal 1: Growing WIP (more started work, not more finished work)

WIP growing is the earliest and most reliable sign that your system is accumulating inventory instead of delivering value.

In Drift, leads keep starting work because it feels like progress. "We'll parallelize." "We can't block people." "We'll finish it later."

But WIP is not neutral. Every additional in-progress item increases:

- coordination cost,
- dependency risk,
- context switching,

- and the chance that something will be reopened after partial integration.

When WIP grows, predictability dies because the team stops finishing and starts juggling.

The key is not the absolute number of cards. The key is whether **your started work keeps expanding while real done throughput stays flat.** That's a system failure, not an individual failure.

A fast corrective action (before you overthink it): **stop starting**. Pick the smallest set of in-progress items that can be finished to integrated done, and put everything else on hold. This is where a WIP cap matters, even if you don't call it that. Your goal is to restore flow, not to keep everyone "utilized."

Then do the cause analysis: why did you keep starting? Missing "done" definition? Dependencies? Priority churn? Hidden rework? The point of the quick action is to buy space for real diagnosis.

Signal 2: Falling close rate of real "done" (integrated + verified)

You specified the strict definition: close rate is "integrated + tested + shippable," not "closed on the board."

This matters because board-closed can be fake. Real done cannot.

In Drift, local closes still happen ("my part is done"), but the integrated close rate falls. Items get stuck in integration, QA, or review. Or they "close" and reopen.

A falling real close rate means your pipeline is clogged. Typical causes:

- integration is late and painful,
- QA surface exploded because changes were unpriced,
- build stability is poor, so verification is slow,
- or priorities keep shifting, so nothing reaches the finish line.

A quick corrective action: **force a finish sprint** (not a new ceremony, just a focus window). For a short period, you prioritize only work that increases real done throughput: integration, bug fixes that unblock acceptance, finishing partially done items. No new features. No new "improvements." Restore the ability to close.

Then you analyze: what is the main choke point – merge/integration, QA bandwidth, unclear acceptance criteria, or recurring rework?

Signal 3: "No builds" (or no usable builds)

This signal is underrated. If you don't have builds, you don't have momentum. You have isolated activity.

And "no builds" doesn't always mean literally no build artifacts. It also means:

- builds exist but are constantly broken,
- builds exist but nobody trusts them,
- builds exist but aren't tested (so regressions hide),
- builds exist but are not frequent enough to give fast feedback.

In Drift, teams work on branches, integrate late, and then spend days chasing merge conflicts and regressions. The project loses the ability to learn quickly. When feedback loops slow down, rework skyrockets. That kills momentum.

To be concrete, so here's what "build reality" looks like when momentum exists:

- a build that can be produced at least daily (often nightly),
- basic automated checks (even minimal smoke tests),
- and a clear definition of "build is green enough to test."

You don't need perfect CI/CD. You need **a reliable feedback loop**.

Quick corrective action: **restore a green baseline.** That may mean temporarily pausing risky merges, focusing on build health tasks, and agreeing on what "green" means (even if it's minimal). If the build is red, nothing else matters, because all progress becomes speculative.

Then analyze: why is build health failing? Too many parallel changes? High-risk surfaces touched without extra verification? Missing gating? Late integration? This is where your "auto-risk thresholds" topic directly connects: if core loop/perf/saves/platform changes are frequent and not treated as risk, build health will collapse.

Signal 4: Priority conflicts (people pulling in different directions)

Priority conflicts are the human-visible symptom that alignment is decaying.

In Drift, design says onboarding is top priority. Tech says performance is top priority. Art says content backlog is top priority. Production says milestone deliverables are top priority. Everyone has a valid argument. But the system has no single "what wins" for the next iteration.

This creates a specific pattern: the team appears active, but efforts cancel out. Work is started and then invalidated. People stop trusting priorities because they change mid-flight.

This is where your earlier decision system matters. Priority conflicts are not resolved by more debate. They are resolved by:

- a clear decider for scope packaging,
- explicit trade-offs,
- and a decision log/backlog update that makes the priority real.

Quick corrective action: **force a one-week priority lock for finishing work**, with one owner accountable for scope packaging. Not forever – just long enough to restore flow. Then run a short re-alignment step: reaffirm pillars and constraints, and restate what wins for the next slice.

Cause analysis: why do priorities conflict? Missing or vague pillars? Hidden stakeholder pressure? Too many goals in one milestone? Lack of "nongoals"? This connects back to your alignment and decision contract chapters for a reason: momentum is downstream of decisions.

Why these signals cluster (and why you should treat them as a system problem)

Growing WIP leads to fewer integrated closes.
Fewer integrated closes reduce trust in planning.
Reduced trust increases priority thrash ("we need to fix everything").
Thrash increases WIP and destabilizes builds.
Bad builds slow feedback, increasing rework, reducing closes further.

It's a loop. That's why early intervention matters. You're not fixing a metric. You're stopping a negative feedback cycle.

A simple "what to do tomorrow" response

When you see these signals, don't start with a workshop. Start with containment:

Restore a green build baseline.
Stop starting new work; finish what's open to real done.
Lock priorities short-term to remove thrash.
Then analyze causes using the lenses you already have: done definition, change pipeline discipline, decision rights, and trade-offs.

That combination – fast containment plus honest diagnosis – is how producers and leads bring momentum back without turning the project into process theater.

III. "Work expands to fill ambiguity" – how uncertainty eats time

In production, time isn't eaten mostly by "hard work." It's eaten by uncertainty.

Not the honest kind ("we don't know yet, so we'll test it"). The dangerous kind: ambiguity that sits in the project like fog. When the target is unclear, work doesn't stop. It expands. People fill the space with assumptions, defensive work, extra options, and endless iteration – because nobody can confidently say "this is done."

That's what this line means in practice: **work expands to fill ambiguity.** Not because people are lazy or inefficient, but because the system forces them to protect themselves.

Focus on design scope, so let's ground it there.

The guiding scenario: a feature that never stabilizes because the goal is unclear

Project Drift again, mid-production. The team wants to "improve combat feel." That sentence sounds normal. It's also a trap.

"Improve combat feel" is not a decision. It's a vibe. It contains no threshold, no trade-off, no success criteria, no non-goals. So the team starts working, because the milestone needs progress.

Design creates a few variants. Then another variant. Then "just one more tweak." Animation adds extra transitions. VFX adds more feedback. UI adjusts numbers. Tech tries to optimize. QA reports inconsistency. The feature keeps moving, but it never lands.

Why? Because without a clear target, every critique is valid and infinite:

- "It's not punchy enough."
- "Too noisy."
- "Too slow."
- "Not readable."
- "Feels floaty."
- "Feels unfair."

Each comment opens a new direction. Work expands to satisfy all of them, because the project has no explicit "what wins" and no explicit "what we will not do."

This is how ambiguity becomes time loss: not as one big failure, but as continuous drift.

The mechanics: where ambiguity turns into time waste

There are four predictable ways design ambiguity eats time.

1) It multiplies options

When the target is unclear, the safest behavior is to keep options alive. Designers don't commit, because committing without criteria is risky. So you get parallel prototypes, variants, and branches. Options feel like progress. They are mostly inventory.

2) It creates rework by invalidating work late

If "combat feel" isn't framed by pillars and constraints, someone will eventually say: "This isn't our game." And they'll be right – because the game was never defined tightly enough. Late invalidation creates rework that looks like "iteration," but behaves like waste.

3) It shifts effort into defensive overproduction

Ambiguity makes people add buffers: extra polish, extra failsafes, extra edge-case handling, extra content. Not because it's needed, but because it might be needed once the goal becomes clearer. That's time spent protecting against unknown future criteria.

4) It prevents "done"

When "done" is vague, people keep touching the feature. Even after it ships to the build, it reopens repeatedly. That destroys momentum: close rate drops, WIP grows, builds destabilize.

The producer/lead lens: ambiguity is a debt that compounds

Design ambiguity feels harmless because it's intangible. But it compounds like debt.

Every day you leave a feature goal ambiguous, you don't just lose one day. You increase:

- the number of interpretations,
- the number of dependencies,
- the number of stakeholder opinions,
- and the amount of work that can be invalidated later.

That's why late-stage "alignment fixes" are expensive. The earlier you reduce ambiguity, the cheaper it is.

This is also why teams confuse motion for momentum. They're working, but they're not converging.

How to fight it without killing creativity

The solution is not "lock design early." That's naive. Games need iteration.

The solution is to convert ambiguity into controlled uncertainty: you explicitly name what you don't know, you timebox it, you define what evidence ends the uncertainty, and you keep the rest stable.

Here are the practical antidotes that fit everything you've built so far.

Antidote 1: Define the win condition for the change (and the non-goal)

Before you iterate, define what "better" means in a way that can converge.

For "combat feel," that could be:

- a pillar-driven target ("readability under stress beats spectacle"),
- a player outcome ("players understand why they got hit"),
- a pacing outcome ("time-to-first-impact under X seconds"),
- or a skill outcome ("high mastery comes from positioning, not twitch").

You don't need perfect metrics. You need **a directional constraint** that tells the team what wins and what loses.

Then define at least one explicit non-goal: what you are not optimizing for right now. This is how you prevent infinite expansion.

Without a non-goal, iteration has no boundary.

Antidote 2: Timebox uncertainty with a spike, not endless iteration

If you genuinely don't know what "good" looks like yet, don't commit to building the feature. Commit to learning.

That's what a spike is for: a short, deliberate effort with a question and exit criteria.

Example structure:

- Question: "Which of these two approaches improves readability without slowing pacing?"
- Timebox: "Two days."
- Exit: "Pick one approach or reject both; write down what was learned."

This turns ambiguity from a swamp into a controlled experiment. It also protects the schedule because it forces a decision point.

Antidote 3: Enforce a decision point with a decider and a trade-off

Design ambiguity often persists because nobody is authorized to end it.

This is where your decision rights and Decision Contract concepts matter. Someone must have the right to say: "We choose A. We stop exploring B. We pay this trade-off. We move on."

If you don't have that, you get consensus theater around taste, and the feature remains permanently "in progress."

A practical habit: when iteration has gone beyond a reasonable timebox, you force a decision meeting with the required inputs: options, costs, risks, pillar impact, and what changes in backlog. No more "we'll keep iterating."

Antidote 4: Tighten "done" for the current phase

Ambiguity feeds on weak done definitions.

If "done" is "implemented," ambiguity will keep pulling the work back. If "done" is "integrated + verified + meets the current success criteria," the feature can actually land.

And once it lands, you protect it from constant reopening by requiring that new changes to it go through the change pipeline (Evaluate ->

Decide -> Communicate). That's how you prevent "just one more tweak" from becoming a lifestyle.

The key mindset shift

You don't manage time by asking people to work faster. You manage time by reducing the space in which work can expand.

Design scope ambiguity is space. It invites endless options, endless revisions, endless opinions.
So the producer/lead job is to constrain it intelligently:

- define what wins,
- define what doesn't matter right now,
- timebox learning,
- and force convergence through owned decisions.

That's how you keep creativity – without letting uncertainty quietly eat your schedule.

IV. Momentum principles: small closures, clear exit criteria, short feedback loops

Momentum is not magic. It's a set of habits that make "done" happen reliably.

In Chapter 5 we defined momentum as steady flow of real done work and predictability. Now we turn that into a practical checklist for leads and producers. Not theory. Not a culture poster. A way to run a project so it keeps finishing.

We'll keep the same guiding project – Project Drift – because it's a useful baseline: busy team, unstable priorities, vague "done," and work that keeps stalling.

The three principles that reliably restore momentum are:

small closures, clear exit criteria, short feedback loops.

They sound simple. They're hard because they force discipline and they expose ambiguity. That's exactly why they work.

Project Drift: why nothing landed

In Drift, items stayed "almost done" for weeks. People started work faster than they finished it. The build was often unusable. Every review uncovered surprises. The team kept reacting.

When you look closer, you see the pattern:

- tasks were too big to close safely,
- nobody agreed what "done" meant for the item,
- and feedback arrived late, so rework was expensive.

Fix those three and momentum comes back.

Principle 1: Small closures (aggressively reduce the size of "done" increments)

If you want momentum, you must treat "big items" as a risk. Big items hide uncertainty, create dependency chains, and stall. They also create the illusion of progress because so many people can be "working on it" while nothing lands.

Small closures mean you structure work so that each unit can become integrated, verified done quickly – ideally in days, not weeks. And yes, that often means your tickets look less "clean" and more "atomic." That's a trade you should happily take, because the real cleanliness is in the build, not in the board taxonomy.

In Drift, "Improve combat feel" became:

- "Add clearer hit feedback for heavy attacks,"
- "Adjust camera shake rules for readability,"
- "Tighten tutorial prompt for stamina indicator,"
- "Tune enemy wind-up audio cues."

Each of those is still meaningful, but each can be closed. Each creates a visible improvement. Each reduces uncertainty.

Leads often resist this because they worry about losing architectural cohesion or design cohesion. The answer is: cohesion comes from pillars, exit criteria, and review cadence – not from oversized work items.

Checklist test: if the item cannot be demoed in a build and verified without a week of coordination, it's too big.

Principle 2: Clear exit criteria (define "what stops the work" before the work starts)

Exit criteria are the antidote to "work expands to fill ambiguity."

Without exit criteria, you don't have an item. You have a conversation. And conversations don't close.

Exit criteria should be qualitative and practical. They should answer: "How will we know this is acceptable and can stop being touched?"

For example, instead of "make tutorial clearer," exit criteria might be:

- "A first-time player can complete the first tutorial step without extra prompts; no soft locks; messaging is consistent with UI state."
- "The new prompt does not introduce new failure states; regression check passes on the onboarding path."

- "The behavior is consistent across the supported input methods/platform contexts we care about right now."

Notice what this does: it prevents endless tweaks, because you're not optimizing for "best possible." You're optimizing for "acceptable under current constraints."

Exit criteria also protect quality and trust. When criteria are clear, QA knows what to verify, leads know what to sign off, and producers can forecast.

Checklist test: if two people in different disciplines would disagree about whether the item is done, your exit criteria are missing.

Principle 3: Short feedback loops (reduce the time between change and reality)

Short feedback loops are what turns small closures into real momentum instead of local "completion."

If you don't see the change quickly in a reliable build, the work is speculative. If you don't test it quickly, defects compound. If you don't review it quickly, it drifts.

In Drift, the team was integrating late and reviewing sporadically. That created a consistent pattern: surprises arrived days later, so fixes were disruptive and demoralizing.

Short feedback loops mean:

- you integrate frequently enough that problems surface early,
- you validate changes in a real build quickly,
- and you keep the review cycle short so work converges.

You don't need perfect CI to benefit. You need a disciplined "reality cadence."

Checklist test: if you regularly discover that "done work" isn't actually usable until much later, your feedback loop is too long.

The lead/producer checklist (how to enforce these principles without bureaucracy)

Here's the enforcement logic in plain language, that works most of the times and is not overwhelming in use:

Start by cutting work smaller than feels comfortable. It will feel "too small" at first. That's normal. It's the point. Your goal is to make closing the default behavior.

Before anyone starts, write exit criteria that would allow a different lead to verify the outcome. If you can't write them, you're not ready to start. That's not gatekeeping – starting without criteria is how you create hidden rework.

Then make sure the feedback loop exists: changes must land in a build quickly, be smoke-tested quickly, and be reviewed quickly. If the build is red, stop pretending you have momentum. Restore build health first.

Finally, protect these habits from priority thrash. Small closures plus frequent feedback only work if work is allowed to finish. If priorities change daily, you'll create a pile of half-closures and churn.

3 concrete practices that create short feedback loops

Here are three that are lightweight and effective in most teams:

Nightly build + minimal smoke test

A daily build that is "green enough to test," plus a small set of checks that catch the obvious regressions. The point is fast detection, not perfect coverage.

Daily or near-daily playtest of the current build

Not a big ceremony. A short, consistent habit. It forces the team to face reality and keeps design changes grounded.

Fast review cadence with a time expectation

If reviews take days, feedback loops break. Set an expectation that critical changes get reviewed quickly, even if that means smaller review chunks (another reason small closures matter).

What changes in Project Drift when these principles are applied

Within a couple of weeks, Drift starts to feel different:

- work lands more often,
- "almost done" shrinks,
- the build becomes more reliable,
- QA load becomes less chaotic,
- and planning starts to regain credibility.

Not because people worked harder. Because the system stopped rewarding large, ambiguous, slow-feedback work.

The blunt takeaway

If you want momentum, you don't need motivation. You need closure.

Small closures make finishing possible.
Exit criteria make stopping legitimate.
Short feedback loops make truth arrive early.

That's the whole engine.

V. Practical KPIs (no vanity): throughput, lead time, interruption count, build stability

Many teams either measure nothing, or they measure everything and still don't know what's happening.

The point of KPIs in production is not reporting. It's steering. If a metric doesn't change your next decision, it's vanity – even if it looks "professional."

So keep this lean: four KPIs that map directly to momentum and predictability, measured per project with strict definitions. You don't need rituals. You need early warnings and obvious actions.

1) Throughput (real "done" per unit time)

Definition: the count of work items that reach your strict "done" definition in a given period (week is usually the cleanest). "Done" here means integrated, verified, and accepted at the current quality bar – not "moved to Done on a board."

Throughput is the simplest truth: are we turning effort into shippable progress?

Why it's not vanity: it's hard to fake without actually finishing. And it's directly connected to predictability.

Suggested alerts:

If throughput drops for two consecutive weeks, or becomes highly erratic (big spike then drought), assume momentum is slipping.

What you do when it triggers:

Don't demand speed. Reduce WIP and increase closure. The corrective action is usually a short focus window on finishing in-progress work (integration, fixing blockers, clarifying exit criteria). If the build is unstable, fix build health first – because throughput depends on being able to verify.

2) Lead time (start -> real done)

Definition: the elapsed time from when an item is started (work begins) to when it becomes real done (integrated + verified). Track the typical value (median) rather than chasing averages, because averages get distorted by outliers.

Lead time is your predictability engine. If you know that "typical items take ~X days," planning becomes real. If lead time drifts upward, your system is accumulating friction.

Suggested alerts:

If median lead time rises for two weeks in a row, or if a growing portion of items take "too long" (whatever "too long" means for your project), treat it as a flow problem.

What you do when it triggers:

Shrink work items aggressively (small closures), tighten exit criteria, and reduce dependencies. Also check for priority churn: stop starting new work and let items finish. Lead time usually inflates when the team is juggling too many partially done things.

3) Interruption count (unplanned priority changes)

Definition: count the number of times in a period (again: week is practical) that the team's committed plan is interrupted by new urgent work or a priority reshuffle that causes active work to stop or be reworked.

This is the KPI that exposes the hidden tax of "we're agile." Interruption count doesn't judge whether interruptions are justified. It shows whether your plan is stable enough to finish anything.

Suggested alerts:

If interruptions happen more than once per week as a norm, you should assume predictability will suffer. If you hit multiple interruptions in a single week, don't pretend it's "just a busy week" – it's a system state.

What you do when it triggers:

First, force trade-offs. Every interruption must displace something explicitly (backlog reality must change). Second, classify interruptions: are they must-fix, compliance, or just "nice-to-have pressure"? If "nice-to-have" is interrupting, your change gate is leaking. This is where the Evaluate -> Decide -> Communicate pipeline stops being optional.

4) Build stability (usable build availability)

Definition: the proportion of time you have a build that is usable for testing and review, plus how often builds are broken or blocked from verification. Keep it simple: "green enough to test" vs "not."

Build stability is the foundation KPI because it affects everything else. If builds are frequently broken or untrustworthy, lead time increases, throughput drops, and interruptions multiply because people scramble to fix fires.

Suggested alerts:

If you can't reliably produce a usable build at least daily (or at your agreed cadence), or if broken builds become "normal," treat it as a critical risk. In late production, your tolerance should be even lower.

What you do when it triggers:

Restore a green baseline. That may mean temporarily pausing risky merges, prioritizing build health tasks, and reducing WIP. You don't "push through" broken build periods without paying a compounding cost.

How these KPIs work together (and why four is enough)

Throughput tells you if you're shipping progress.
Lead time tells you if you're predictable.
Interruption count tells you if your plan is being respected.
Build stability tells you if feedback loops are functioning.

If any of these degrade, you already know what kind of action to take – without introducing a dashboard religion.

A minimal operating stance (so this doesn't become measurement theatre)

Measure weekly. Look at trend, not single data points. Trigger actions only when the trend is clear (two-week signal is usually enough). Keep definitions strict and consistent. And most importantly: don't use these metrics to judge people. Use them to detect when the system is drifting into chaos.

If you do that, these four KPIs become what they should be: a small set of instruments that keep momentum honest.

VI. Behavioral red flags: heroics, overtime, "almost done" forever, missing ownership

Behavioral red flags are what you see before the charts catch up.

A producer or lead can look at throughput, lead time, interruptions, build stability – and still miss the fact that the team is already slipping into a bad state. Because people compensate. They push harder. They patch holes with personal effort. The project looks like it's "holding," until it suddenly isn't.

So treat these behaviors as early warning signals. Not as moral failures. As system symptoms.

We'll keep Project Drift as the guiding scenario. Mid-production, constant pressure, unclear "done," priorities shifting. The team is busy. The KPI trends start to wobble, but not enough to trigger panic yet. And then the behaviors appear.

Red flag 1: Heroics (the project runs on a few "savers")

Heroics is when progress depends on individuals repeatedly doing extraordinary effort to keep the project moving – late nights, weekend fixes, "I'll just handle it," firefighting integrations.

In the short term, heroics can be necessary. Sometimes there's a real incident: a broken build before a milestone review, a submission blocker, a corrupted save path. You fix it. That's normal.

It becomes a red flag when heroics turns into a pattern: the same few people are always the glue, and the plan quietly assumes they will keep being the glue.

That directly connects to your KPIs:

- throughput may stay temporarily stable because the "heroes" are pushing closure through,
- lead time often worsens for everyone else (because the system is chaotic and heroes are interrupt-driven),
- interruption count rises (fires create fires),

- build stability becomes dependent on one person's availability.

What to do next: make heroics explicit and bounded. If a heroics event happens, treat it like a production incident:

- capture what triggered it (root cause),
- decide what you change so it doesn't repeat (process gate, definition of done, integration cadence),
- and enforce recovery (time off, reduced load) so you don't convert "save the milestone" into "burn the team."

If you can't name the system change after a heroics event, you're just normalizing it.

Red flag 2: Overtime becomes normal (not occasional)

Overtime is a blunt instrument. It creates an illusion of progress because you see hours and activity. But it usually damages the thing you actually need: predictable flow.

In Drift, overtime starts as "just this week." Then it becomes "until we catch up." That "catch up" moment never arrives because the underlying causes – unclear done and priority thrash – continue to create rework.

In KPI terms, overtime often correlates with:

- throughput not improving proportionally (more hours, same closures),
- lead time not shrinking (items still stall; you're just tired while they stall),
- build stability getting worse (fatigue increases mistakes; firefighting merges),
- interruptions increasing (people stop coordinating well and create secondary issues).

Overtime also hides the true cost of decisions. It turns missing trade-offs into human debt.

What to do next: treat overtime as a signal that the plan is lying. The corrective action is not "rest harder." It's structural:

- reduce WIP and stop starting new work,
- lock priorities short-term so things can finish,
- shrink items into small closures,

- and restore build stability so feedback loops are reliable.

If you don't change the system, telling people to stop overtime is just a guilt trip.

Red flag 3: "Almost done" forever (permanent near-finish)

This is one of the cleanest behavioral signals of momentum loss. People say "it's 90%," "just polish," "just a few bugs," week after week.

"Almost done" forever usually means one of three things:

- exit criteria are unclear, so the finish line keeps moving,
- integration/QA is the real work and nobody planned for it,
- or priorities keep changing, so the item keeps being reopened.

This maps directly to lead time and churn. Your lead time inflates because items don't reach real done. Your throughput drops because closures aren't real. Your interruption count increases because "almost done" items become convenient targets for last-minute changes.

What to do next: force convergence. Pick one "almost done" item and do a hard intervention:

- write explicit exit criteria that match integrated, verified done,
- identify the actual blockers (integration, missing assets, unclear acceptance),
- stop allowing new changes to that item until it closes,
- and timebox the remaining work to closure, not to "improvement."

If you can't close one representative "almost done" item, you don't have a delivery problem on that item – you have a system problem.

Red flag 4: Missing ownership (no decider, so work floats)

You chose "missing ownership" primarily as lack of decider. That's the correct lens here.

When there is no decider, the team will still work. But they will work in a way that maximizes safety for themselves:

- they keep options open,
- they avoid committing to trade-offs,
- they defer hard calls,
- and they wait for "someone" to clarify direction.

That creates invisible delays. People don't say "we're blocked." They just slow down, because pushing forward without decision authority is risky.

On the KPI side, missing decider often looks like:

- growing WIP (people start partial work while waiting for a decision),
- rising lead time (items stall at decision points),
- more interruptions (decisions happen late, causing rework),
- instability in throughput (closures depend on who finally makes a call).

What to do next: assign the decider and make it visible. Not for everything – specifically for decisions that affect scope, pillars, quality, and priority packaging. Then enforce the rule you've already established: the only path for meaningful change is Evaluate -> Decide -> Communicate. If the decider isn't named, the decision doesn't happen, and the change doesn't enter the committed plan.

This also reduces politics. When decision rights are explicit, people stop lobbying in DMs because it stops working.

Why these behaviors matter more than they seem

Heroics and overtime can make a project look healthy while it's actually bleeding predictability.

"Almost done" forever and missing decider can make a project look "careful" while it's actually stuck in ambiguity.

All four are early signals that the system is compensating for weak structure. If you ignore them, your KPIs will degrade next. If you respond early, you can restore momentum without a crisis.

The producer/lead stance is simple and direct:

If your plan requires heroics, it's not a plan.
If overtime is normal, your scope is lying.
If "almost done" is permanent, your done definition is fake.
If there's no decider, work will expand to fill ambiguity.

Treat the behavior as a warning, then fix the system that makes the behavior necessary.

VII. Interventions in 48h / 2 weeks / 1 month (what you can realistically fix on each horizon)

When momentum collapses late in production, people reach for big solutions: "We need a new process," "We need a new tool," "We need a reorg."

That's almost always the wrong instinct. Late production doesn't reward reinvention. It rewards **containment, clarity, and finishing**.

You chose a late-production scenario and the primary pain source: **lack of a real definition of done**. That's exactly the kind of problem that looks abstract, but creates very concrete disasters: "almost done forever," unstable builds, churn, and panic.

The key is being honest about time horizons. In 48 hours you can stop bleeding and regain control of reality. In two weeks you can restore a steady "done" flow. In a month you can rebuild predictability and make it harder to relapse. You cannot "fix culture" in any of these horizons. You can, however, change the system so the culture doesn't need heroics to survive.

The core rule across all horizons

Before we split by timeframe, one rule that makes everything else coherent:

Nothing is done unless it is integrated, verified, and accepted at the current quality bar.

You can still have intermediate states ("implementation done," "content done"), but you must stop calling them done. Late production is not the time for semantic ambiguity. Your plan cannot be built on wishful labels.

Everything below is designed to make that definition real.

In 48 hours: stop the bleeding and make "done" visible

In 48 hours you are not redesigning the project. You are stabilizing it. Your goal is to create a single reality and prevent more partial work from piling up.

First, **freeze "new work" intake** for anything that isn't a true must-fix or compliance blocker. This isn't a philosophical stance. It's a practical one: if "done" is unclear, starting new work is how you create more inventory and more uncertainty.

Second, **pick a small number of near-finished items and force closure** using the strict done definition. Not "we'll try." Force it: integrate, verify, accept. If an item cannot be closed quickly, it's not "almost done." It's a hidden scope item. Admit that and treat it accordingly.

Third, **write exit criteria for those few items** in plain language. Late production is full of "polish" traps. Exit criteria are how you stop the work from expanding. Keep them qualitative but testable: what must be true in the build for this to be considered done?

Fourth, **restore a usable build baseline** if build stability is shaky. You don't need to build a perfect pipeline. You need a build that can be tested today. If the build is red or untrustworthy, your "done" definition is impossible to apply because nothing can be verified.

Finally, **make the plan truthful**: update the backlog so the team can see what is truly committed versus what is paused. Late production rumor cycles are deadly. Truth is a stabilizer.

What you can realistically fix in 48 hours is not "momentum." It's **control**: fewer active items, clearer finish lines, and a build that can validate reality.

In 2 weeks: rebuild flow by making "done" enforceable and repeatable

Two weeks is enough time to change how work finishes, which is the real lever for momentum. This is where you turn your strict done definition into a working system rather than a slogan.

Start by **standardizing a minimal definition of done per work type**. You don't need a book. You need a few consistent rules that everyone can apply:

- integrated into the main line,
- verified in a testable build,
- meets exit criteria,
- no known critical regressions introduced,
- any required follow-ups (docs, decision log link, etc.) are attached if applicable.

Then **reduce WIP structurally**, not heroically. Keep the team finishing. If you let people keep starting new tasks, lead time will explode and "almost done" will return. Two weeks of low WIP and high closure can dramatically change project feel.

Next, **run a focused "closure cadence."** This doesn't mean ceremonies. It means you regularly ask one question in leads sync: "What closes this week, in the build, by the strict definition?" If you can't answer, you're still living in ambiguity.

Also, **clean up the backlog language.** A lot of "done" confusion is actually ticket ambiguity: tasks written as vague desires instead of testable outcomes. In two weeks, you can rewrite the worst offenders into exit-criteria-shaped tickets and stop the expansion of work through interpretation.

If you consider adding lightweight smoke tests or basic build checks, this is the time – **but only if they directly support the strict done definition**. If tests will take time and won't reduce reopens or build breakage, they're a distraction. Late production tooling changes must pay back fast.

What you can realistically fix in two weeks is **steady closure**: throughput improves, lead time starts shrinking, and the build becomes a place where work actually finishes.

In 1 month: restore predictability and make relapse harder

A month is long enough to move from "we can finish" to "we can forecast." This is where you harden the system so momentum doesn't collapse again under pressure.

The first move is to **stabilize decision boundaries around change**. Late production often dies from "last-minute improvements." In a month you can enforce the rule that any scope/quality-impacting change must go through Evaluate -> Decide -> Communicate, with explicit trade-offs. This protects “done” from being reopened casually.

Second, you can **align the team on a small set of exit-criteria patterns** for recurring work: bug fixes, tuning, UI adjustments, content integration. You’re not creating bureaucracy; you’re creating shared standards so work closes consistently.

Third, you can **connect the practical KPIs to action** in a lightweight way:

- if throughput wobbles, reduce WIP and focus on closures,
- if lead time creeps up, shrink items and tighten exit criteria,
- if interruptions rise, enforce trade-offs and stop DM commitments,
- if build stability drops, restore green baseline immediately.

The value of a month horizon is not better reporting. It’s **faster correction** when the system drifts.

Finally, use the month to **pay down the specific ambiguity debt that keeps regenerating “almost done.”** This often means clarifying a few core acceptance standards (visual quality thresholds, performance expectations, platform requirements, save integrity rules). You don’t need perfection. You need fewer arguments about what “good enough” means.

What you can realistically fix in one month is **predictability**: fewer surprise reopens, more stable close rate, clearer trade-offs, and a project that behaves consistently enough to plan.

The honest takeaway

- In **48 hours**, you can stop the chaos: freeze intake, close a few items by strict done, restore a usable build, and make the plan truthful.
- In **2 weeks**, you can restore momentum: enforce “done,” reduce WIP, and create repeatable closure.
- In **1 month**, you can restore predictability: harden change gates, standardize exit criteria patterns, and connect KPIs to real corrective actions.

If you try to do the 1-month work in 48 hours, you'll create process noise and still fail to ship. If you do the 48-hour containment work properly, the longer fixes become possible without panic.

CHAPTER 6:
Templates
(one-pager, pillars/constraints, decision contract starter)

I. Template: Project One-Pager (required fields + an example fill)

A good one-pager is not a summary. It's a **control panel**.

It exists so the whole team can answer the same questions the same way, without meetings, without guesswork, and without "someone said." In pre-production, that matters more than pretty decks. A one-pager is the smallest artifact that can actually reduce chaos – because it forces ownership, priorities, and trade-offs to exist in a visible, durable form.

Below is a **minimal template** (lean enough to fit on one page if you're disciplined, but allowed to spill to a second page if you keep it dense in meaning). After that you'll get an example fill that is "universal" (no genre-specific fluff).

Required fields (the minimal set that matters)

1) Project snapshot

- Project name (working title)
- Team size & key roles (just the leads/owners, not org charts)
- Target platforms (and any hard platform constraints)
- Target release window (rough) + next milestone date
- Current phase (pre-prod scope definition / prototype validation / vertical slice)

2) The win condition (what "wins" in this phase)

One sentence. If you can't say it, you're not aligned.

3) Pillars (3–5 max)

Short, testable statements. Not values like "fun." Pillars should help you say no.

4) Constraints (hard limits that shape decisions)

Time, budget/runway sensitivity (light, but honest), technical/platform constraints, content constraints.

5) Nongoals (explicit "we will NOT do")

3–7 items. These are your scope creep shield.

6) Scope boundary (what is in / what is out for the next milestone)

A small list of the must-have deliverables for the next milestone, plus explicit exclusions if needed.

7) Definition of Done (for the milestone)

One short block describing what "done" means for milestone acceptance (integrated, verified, quality bar). Keep it strict.

8) Decision and change gate (the minimum rule)

- "A change that affects scope/pillars/quality must go through: Evaluate -> Decide -> Communicate."
- Where the decision record lives (decision log location)
  Keep it short. The point is to make "DM decisions" non-real.

9) Top risks & unknowns (with immediate next actions)

3–5 items max. Each risk must have a next step (often a timeboxed spike).

10) Communication basics (where truth lives)

Where to find:

- latest one-pager version,
- the plan/backlog,
- the build,
- and how decisions/changes are communicated (channel + cadence, minimal).

That's the template. If you add more, you're probably adding noise unless the team is genuinely blocked without it.

Example fill (universal, pre-production)

1) Project snapshot

Project: *Project Northstar* (working title)
Team: 18 total. Leads: Design (A), Engineering (B), Art (C), Production (D).
Platforms: PC first. Console considered post-launch (not in current scope).
Release window: Target: H2 next year (subject to vertical slice outcome).
Next milestone: Vertical Slice readiness check – 10 weeks from kickoff.
Phase: Pre-prod: validate core loop + production feasibility.

2) Win condition (this phase)

By the end of the vertical slice, we can show a repeatable 15–20 minute experience that is clearly "our game," runs within budget, and can be produced at scale.

3) Pillars (3–5)

1. **Readable under pressure:** the player always understands what happened and why.
2. **Meaningful choices, not busywork:** decisions change outcomes, not just numbers.
3. **Fast iteration:** features must be buildable and tunable without weeks of re-work.
4. **Stable feel over novelty:** we prefer consistent quality over constant new mechanics.

4) Constraints

- **Time:** Vertical slice is a hard gate in 10 weeks (scope must fit).
- **Budget/runway:** No assumption of extra hires during slice; scope must fit current team.
- **Technical:** Must maintain a playable build at least daily; no "integration at the end."
- **Content:** Content creation must be scalable (avoid bespoke content that can't be repeated).

5) Nongoals (for pre-prod + slice)

- No online/multiplayer features.
- No procedural generation beyond simple parameters (if any).
- No platform certification work (PC only for slice).
- No complex meta progression/economy systems.
- No "cinematic story pipeline" (minimal narrative framing only).
- No new toolchain investments unless they pay back within the slice timeframe.

6) Scope boundary (next milestone deliverables)

In (must-have for slice):

- Core loop playable end-to-end (start -> decision -> consequence -> feedback).
- One representative level/segment with final-quality "feel" (not final art volume).

- One representative enemy/challenge type + one variation.
- UI pass sufficient for readability (not final styling).
- Basic save/load if required by loop (otherwise explicitly out).

Out (explicit):

- Additional content variety (more levels, more enemies, more items).
- Full tutorialization and accessibility suite (only minimal onboarding).
- Full audio/VO pipeline (placeholder acceptable if readable).

7) Definition of Done (vertical slice)

A slice item is "done" only when it is integrated into the main build, verified in the daily build, meets the slice acceptance criteria (pillar-aligned), and does not introduce known critical regressions. If it can't be tested in the build, it isn't done.

8) Decision and change gate

Any change affecting **scope, pillars, quality, or milestone deliverables** must go through: **Evaluate -> Decide -> Communicate.**

Decision record lives in: a shared decision log linked from the backlog. A change is not real until backlog and decision record are updated (no DM approvals).

9) Top risks & unknowns (with next actions)

1. **Core loop clarity risk:** we might not reach "readable under pressure."
   Next action: 3-day prototype test focusing on feedback/readability; decide on approach.
2. **Production scalability risk:** content may be too expensive per unit.
   Next action: define one "content unit" and estimate production cost; adjust scope.
3. **Performance risk:** target hardware performance unknown early.
   Next action: establish a simple performance budget and test in representative scene.
4. **Scope drift risk:** "nice-to-haves" creep into slice.
   Next action: enforce nongoals + require explicit trade-offs for any additions.

10) Communication basics (where truth lives)

- One-pager: stored in shared docs; version/date at top; updated on major decisions.
- Backlog: single source of truth for committed scope.
- Build: daily playable build; if build is broken, restoring it is priority.
- Change communication: decisions posted to the main team channel with link to backlog + decision log; impacted people tagged.

Two practical notes (so this stays "one pager" quality, not "one pager theater")

1. **Keep it updated or delete it.** A stale one-pager is worse than none because it creates false confidence.
2. **Treat it as a decision artifact.** Every field exists to help you make trade-offs. If a field doesn't help decisions, remove it.

II. Template: Pillars / Constraints / Nongoals (format + a "does it work?" test)

In pre-production you don't need more words. You need **better levers**.

Pillars, constraints, and nongoals are those levers. If they're good, they reduce arguments and make trade-offs faster. If they're vague, they become wallpaper – nice-sounding text that doesn't change the backlog.

Below are three minimal templates (separate, lean) and a quick "does it work?" test you can run in 10 minutes with leads.

1) Pillars template (3 max)

Format

Write each pillar as a decision rule, not as a value.

Pillar #1: *[We optimize for X over Y]*
Meaning in practice: *[One sentence: what it changes in choices]*
Example "YES" decision: *[A choice we would approve because of this pillar]*
Example "NO" decision: *[A choice we would reject because of this pillar]*
Keep pillars to **3** unless your project is unusually complex. The point is to create a shared compass, not a manifesto.

Bad vs good pillars

Bad pillars are untestable or universally true.

Bad:

- "Fun."
- "High quality."
- "Immersive."
- "Unique."

They don't help you decide anything because nobody can argue against them.

Good (testable, comparative, directional):

- "Readable under pressure beats spectacle."
- "Player choice beats content volume."
- "Fast iteration beats bespoke solutions."
- "Consistency beats novelty (for this phase)."

These imply trade-offs. That's the whole point.

Does it work? (quick test)

Take two typical conflicts and ask: do we get a clear direction without a long debate?

Test A: UX vs performance

Proposal: "Add heavier UI animations and richer effects in menus." Ask: Which pillar decides? If your pillar is "Readable under pressure beats spectacle," it might allow it only if it doesn't reduce clarity or frame pacing. If your pillar is "Performance stability beats visual polish," it's an easy no. If you can't tell, the pillar is too vague.

Test B: Art vs runtime

Proposal: "Increase texture resolution across the board to improve look." If your pillar says "Consistency beats novelty," you likely prefer stable performance over a global upgrade. If the pillar says "Visual identity is primary," you might accept but demand a scoped version (only hero assets). If the pillar doesn't guide you, it's not doing its job.

2) Constraints template (5 max)

Constraints are not preferences. They're the walls your project will crash into if you ignore them.

Format

Each constraint should be written as: *hard limit + what it means for decisions.*

Constraint: *[Hard limit]*
So we will: *[Decision implication]*
So we will not: *[Boundary]*

Examples of constraint types (pick only what matters now): timebox to vertical slice, budget/runway reality, platform requirements, performance budgets, content production capacity, team skill/tooling limits.

Bad vs good constraints

Bad constraints are generic or unenforced.

Bad:

- "We should be careful with scope."
- "We should optimize performance."
- "We should avoid crunch."

Good:

- "Vertical slice in 10 weeks, no extension assumed -> anything not essential to slice is out."
- "Playable build must exist daily -> no long-lived branches and no late integration."
- "Content must be repeatable by the team we have -> avoid bespoke content that needs specialist production."

Does it work? (quick test)

Test A: Fun vs milestone

Proposal: "Add a new feature that improves the core loop, but needs 3–4 weeks."
If you have a constraint "vertical slice in 10 weeks," the answer becomes: only if it replaces something else. If you can't force that tradeoff, the constraint is not real.

Test B: Platform compliance

Proposal: "Leave platform-specific edge cases for later."
If your constraint says "PC-only for slice," you can defer. If you're already targeting console submission soon, the constraint should force earlier compliance work. If your constraints can't tell you which, they're missing.

3) Nongoals template (5 max)

Nongoals are where you win against scope creep. They are not negativity. They are clarity.

Format

Write nongoals as explicit exclusions with scope boundary.

We will NOT do: *[Feature/system/content]*
Reason: *[What it protects: timebox/pillar/constraint]*
Revisit condition: *[When it may come back – milestone/date/evidence]*

Keep it to **5**. More than that usually means you're trying to compensate for unclear scope.

Bad vs good nongoals

Bad nongoals are vague or absolute without context.

Bad:

- "No scope creep."
- "No more features."
- "No bugs."
- "No multiplayer ever." (unless you truly mean it)

Good:

- "No online/multiplayer in vertical slice (protects timebox + build stability). Revisit after slice if retention goals require it."
- "No procedural generation beyond basic parameter variation (protects iteration speed). Revisit only if content scalability fails."
- "No new toolchain investment unless it pays back within the slice (protects runway/time). Revisit after slice if production scalability is proven."

Does it work? (quick test)

Test A: "It's just a small change"

Proposal: "Can we add a light meta-progression layer? It's small." If you have a nongoal "No meta progression/economy in slice," the answer is immediate: not now. If you can't say no cleanly, you don't have real nongoals.

Test B: Art vs runtime

Proposal: "Let's add more unique enemy variants for variety." If you have a nongoal "No content volume expansion during slice," the team is forced to spend effort on quality and finish instead of breadth. That protects momentum.

How to evolve these after pre-production

Pre-prod pillars/constraints/nongoals are about **convergence**: proving the core loop and feasibility. Later, they change shape:

- **Mid-production:** pillars remain mostly stable, constraints become more operational (performance budgets, content throughput, platform requirements), and nongoals become your scope shield against "nice-to-have pressure."
- **Late production:** constraints tighten (build stability, certification, regression risk), and nongoals often become explicit "no new features" and "only must-fix/compliance/polish within budget," because finishing becomes the win condition.

The mistake is keeping pre-prod text unchanged while the project phase changes. The documents must adapt, or they become theatre.

The 10-minute "does it work?" session (recommended)

Pick **two conflicts** (UX vs perf, art vs runtime, fun vs milestone/cert, scope vs deadline). Run them through pillars/constraints/nongoals. If the group still debates for 15 minutes without a clear direction, your wording is not doing its job. Rewrite until it does.

That's the standard: if it doesn't change decisions, it doesn't belong on the page.

III. Template: Decision Contract Starter (roles, inputs, record format, escalation)

A Decision Contract is not corporate overhead. It's a stress reducer.

In a 30+ person team, decisions don't fail because people are stupid. They fail because **nobody knows what "counts" as a decision**, who has the right to make it, what inputs are required, and where to find the outcome later. That's how you get shadow decisions, surprise vetoes, "we agreed... right?", and a backlog that doesn't match reality.

This starter is intentionally minimal. It's meant to be adopted fast and improved later. The rule is simple: **DM can be discussion, but not decision.** Decisions must leave a durable trail.

Below is a template you can copy into your project docs and fill in.

Decision Contract Starter (fill-in template)

1) Scope and purpose (what this contract covers)

Applies to decisions about:

- **Scope** (what we build / cut / defer, and milestone packaging)
- **Pillars** (what "wins" when trade-offs appear)
- **Tech** (architecture choices that affect delivery, performance, maintainability)

Not intended for: day-to-day micro choices that don't change scope/pillars/tech direction.

Rule of reality: a decision is real only when it is recorded and communicated. Until then it's a proposal.

2) Role model (simple, not corporate)

We use four roles per decision:

- **Decider** – makes the call and owns the outcome.

- **Recommender** – frames options and recommends one.
- **Contributors** – provide inputs (costs, risks, constraints, impacts).
- **Informed** – must know the outcome because it changes their work.

Default assignments by decision type (edit to fit your project):

- **Scope decisions:** Decider = [Project Owner / Game Director / Product Owner]; Recommender = Producer
- **Pillars decisions:** Decider = [Creative Owner]; Recommender = Producer (ensures clarity + tests)
- **Tech decisions:** Decider = Tech Lead; Recommender = Senior Engineer / Tech Lead; Producer ensures impact/trade-off is explicit

Producer's standing responsibility (always on): ensure the decision is decision-ready (inputs exist), recorded, tied to backlog, and communicated to impacted people.

3) Required inputs (what must exist before a "YES/NO")

No heavy forms. Just the minimum to prevent guessing.

Every decision proposal must include:

- **Options** (at least 2 if possible: A vs B; "do nothing" counts as an option)
- **Cost** (rough: time/people, not false precision)
- **Risks** (what can break / what we might learn too late)
- **Impact on pillars** (which pillar it supports or violates, explicitly)
- **Impact on scope** (what changes in committed work; what gets cut/deferred)
- **Tech impact** (especially for scope changes that affect architecture/perf/build stability)

If inputs are missing, the default response is: **"Not ready to decide. Bring it back decision-ready."**

4) Decision record (minimal format + where it lives)

A decision record is a short entry that answers "what did we decide, and why?"

Record format (copy/paste):

- **Decision:** (one sentence)
- **Date:**
- **Decider:**
- **Recommender:**
- **Context:** (what triggered it)
- **Options considered:** (A/B + "do nothing" if relevant)
- **Trade-off:** (what we cut/defer/accept as cost)
- **Impacts:** (scope, pillars, tech – short, factual)
- **Consequences / follow-ups:** (what must be updated next)
- **Links:** (backlog items, doc, prototype, build notes)

Where it lives (choose what fits, but follow these rules):

- If decisions are frequent and tightly tied to tasks: keep records **linked from the backlog** (each decision links to affected items).
- If decisions are fewer but broader: keep a **single decision log document** and link from backlog items to the relevant entry.
- If the team struggles with "nobody reads docs": bias toward **backlog-first**, because tickets are where work actually happens.

Non-negotiable: wherever it lives, it must be easy to find, and the latest decisions must be visible without archaeology.

5) Communication rule (so decisions stop being rumors)

DM is allowed for discussion, alignment, and prep.
DM is not allowed as the final decision channel.

A decision is "released" only when:

- the record exists,
- the backlog is updated (if scope is affected),
- and an announcement is posted in the team's durable channel with a link to the record.

If the decision changes someone's work, they must be considered **impacted** and explicitly informed.

6) Escalation paths (two tracks, kept boring)

Escalation exists so decisions don't rot in limbo. Limbo is where momentum dies.

Escalation is triggered when:

- the decision blocks progress for > [X] working days, or
- the conflict is cross-domain and cannot be resolved by the decider in-track, or
- the decision risks violating pillars/constraints, or
- the trade-off affects external commitments (milestone, platform, contract).

Path A: Scope / Pillars escalation

1. Decider (scope/pillars) attempts resolution with inputs
2. If still blocked: escalate to [Project Owner / Studio Head / Exec Sponsor]
3. If external commitment is impacted: include [Publisher / External Stakeholder] as informed or as decider per contract

Path B: Tech escalation

1. Tech Decider attempts resolution with inputs
2. If still blocked: escalate to [Head of Engineering / Technical Director]
3. If it impacts scope/milestone: loop in Producer + Scope Decider for explicit trade-off

Escalation format (keep it short):

- One page / one message: the decision statement, options, costs, risks, recommended option, and the explicit trade-off. No debates. No history dumps. Just decision-ready inputs.

7) Operating rules (small but critical)

- **No decision without a named decider.** If the decider isn't known, you don't "half-decide." You assign the decider first.

- **One decision = one owner.** Commit clarity beats shared accountability theatre.
- **Trade-offs must be explicit for scope changes.** "We'll figure it out later" is not a trade-off.
- **Decisions must update reality.** If backlog/docs don't change, the decision didn't happen.
- **Reversibility note:** if a decision is hard to reverse (core loop, saves, perf, platform), require stronger inputs and verification steps.

Example fill (short, realistic)

Team size: 45
Scope Decider: Game Director
Pillars Decider: Game Director
Tech Decider: Tech Lead
Recommender for scope/pillars: Producer
Decision record home: Backlog-linked decision log doc (one master doc + links from tickets)
Escalation thresholds: blocked > 2 working days, or impacts milestone commitment

Decision record example:
Decision: "No new meta progression in vertical slice."
Date: 2026-12-01
Decider: Game Director
Recommender: Producer
Context: Proposal to add persistent upgrades to increase engagement.
Options: A) Add basic meta progression now. B) Defer to post-slice. C) Do nothing.
Trade-off: If A, we must cut one core slice deliverable; risk to schedule and build stability increases.
Impacts: Pillars (fast iteration, readability) at risk; scope expands; tech risk moderate.
Outcome: Choose B. Defer.
Follow-ups: Update backlog; add explicit nongoal; communicate decision with link.

IV. "Ready to decide" and "ready to communicate" checklists

These two checklists exist for one reason: to stop you from paying the "soft decision tax."

A decision that happens without inputs becomes a debate later. A decision that gets announced without updating reality becomes a rumor. Both are expensive, especially in a 30+ person team.

Keep these checklists short and practical. They're not meant to gate every small choice. They're meant to gate decisions that affect **scope, pillars, or tech direction.**

I'll give you one base checklist for each, plus small add-ons depending on decision type. "Recommended" means you should do it most of the time. "Stop-rule" means you don't proceed.

Checklist A: Ready to Decide

Use this before a decision meeting or before a decider makes a call.

Stop-rule: If there is no named **Decider**, it is not ready to decide.

Base (6–8 items):

1. **Decider is named** and available to make the call.
2. **Decision statement is one sentence** (what exactly are we deciding).
3. **At least two options exist** (including "do nothing / defer" if that's real).
4. **Rough cost is stated** (time/people, no false precision).
5. **Key risks are listed** (what can break, what can be learned too late).
6. **Trade-off is explicit** (if we say yes, what moves/cuts; if we say no, what we accept).
7. **Impact on pillars/constraints is stated** (which pillar it supports or violates).
8. **Impacted parties are identified** (who will have to change work if this goes through).

Add-ons (only if relevant):

- **Scope decision add-on:** affected backlog items are identified (what gets added/removed/moved).
- **Pillars decision add-on:** one "YES" and one "NO" example exists (so it's testable).
- **Tech decision add-on:** integration and build impact are stated (does this change build stability/perf/saves/platform surfaces).

If you consistently fail this checklist, don't "try harder." Shrink the decisions. Use timeboxed spikes to convert unknowns into inputs.

Checklist B: Ready to Communicate

Use this after a decision is made, before you announce it beyond the decision circle.

Stop-rule: If you can't state the decision and the trade-off in plain language, it is not ready to communicate.

Base (6–8 items):

1. **Decision statement is clear** (what changes, in one sentence).
2. **Reason is clear** (why now, one sentence; no essays).
3. **Trade-off/consequence is stated** (what moved/cut/accepted as cost).
4. **Next actions are explicit** (what people should do differently starting now).
5. **Impacted people/groups are listed** (who must know because their work changes).
6. **Owner for follow-ups is named** (who updates/ensures it sticks).
7. **Q/A boundary is set** (what is decided vs what is still open, if anything).
8. **Single "source of truth" link exists** (recommended: decision record + affected work items).

Recommended reality updates (do these unless you have a good reason not to):

- Update the **backlog** to reflect the new reality (scope/priority changes).
- Update the **decision record** (even minimal).

- Update the **one-pager** if pillars/constraints/nongoals changed.

This is the discipline that kills rumors: the announcement points to reality, not to someone's memory.

How to use these without turning them into bureaucracy

Run "Ready to Decide" as a quick pre-check: if one item is missing, either fill it quickly or explicitly defer. Don't fake it.

Run "Ready to Communicate" as the release gate: decisions aren't "done" until they are communicated in a way that changes behavior. If you skip the release gate, you don't save time – you just postpone the cost and multiply confusion.

If you want one practical habit: treat each decision like a tiny ship. "Ready to decide" is pre-flight. "Ready to communicate" is release. Without both, the work will drift back into ambiguity.

V. Minimal decision log format for Notion / Confluence / Google Doc

A decision log is not there to "document everything." It exists to prevent two expensive failures:

- People re-litigate the same decision six weeks later because nobody remembers the trade-off.
- The backlog drifts away from reality because decisions live in chat.

So keep it minimal, but real. **One decision = one entry.** Start simple, then extend only if it proves useful.

Something that works in Notion/Confluence/Google Docs, includes a **revisit/reversal** field, supports **links when applicable**, and is **maintained by leads** while still being visible to the wider team. Here's the version that survives real production.

Where it lives and how it's used

Audience: Leads maintain it. Everyone should know it exists and what it's for. The broader team can be read-only, or just treat it as "available when needed."

Accountability: The producer is accountable for making sure decisions get logged and tied back to execution reality (backlog / one-pager / build notes) when relevant. The Decider/Recommender supplies the content; the producer ensures it actually becomes an entry.

Shape: Use a single place that is easy to link and easy to scan. The worst decision log is one people avoid because it feels heavy or scattered.

Practical default:

- Notion: a database table (each row can optionally open into a page later).
- Confluence: a single table on a page (plus anchors/links if needed).
- Google Docs: a table at the top of the doc, with optional section headers below.

Option A: Decision Cards (best for print + simple tools)

Tables are great in tools, but they don't always translate well into a book or a simple doc. The clean alternative is a **Decision Card**: a short, scannable block with a fixed structure.

DECISION [ID] – [Date]
Decision: (one sentence)
Type: scope / pillars / tech *(optional but recommended)*
Decider:
Recommender: *(optional)*
Why (context): (one sentence)
Trade-off / cost: (what we give up / what moves)
Impact: (scope/pillars/tech – short)
Links / references: *(if applicable)*
Revisit / reversal condition: (when to re-check, or what evidence would change it)
Status: active / superseded *(optional)*

That's enough. If you can't fill these fields quickly, the decision wasn't "ready to decide."

Example cards (simple, realistic):

DECISION D-017 – 2026-12-04
Decision: No meta-progression in the vertical slice.
Type: Scope
Decider: Game Director
Why (context): The slice must prove the core loop first.
Trade-off / cost: If we add it, we cut one slice deliverable; schedule risk increases.
Impact: Scope reduced; focus on core loop clarity.
Links / references: VS-122, VS-140
Revisit / reversal condition: After slice review, if retention goal is not met.
Status: Active

DECISION D-018 – 2026-12-06
Decision: Pillar updated: "Readable under pressure beats spectacle."
Type: Pillars
Decider: Game Director
Why (context): UX/VFX feedback loops conflict under combat pressure.
Trade-off / cost: Limits polish changes that reduce readability.
Impact: Drives combat/UI decisions and VFX priorities.
Links / references: One-pager v3
Revisit / reversal condition: If target audience changes or readability is consistently solved.
Status: Active

DECISION D-019 – 2026-12-08
Decision: Use a single authoritative save format (approach B).
Type: Tech
Decider: Tech Lead
Why (context): Reduce late-stage migration risk and instability.
Trade-off / cost: More upfront integration work now.
Impact: Less late rework; affects build verification sequencing.
Links / references: Tech note + related tasks
Revisit / reversal condition: Only if performance/memory constraints break the approach.
Status: Active

This format stays compact in a book and still maps cleanly to any tool.

Option B (tool-first): Minimal Table (best inside Notion/Confluence)

If your primary goal is filtering/sorting/searching, the table is still the best operational format. Use it in tools; don't force it into print.

Columns (minimal but complete), ordered by importance:

- **ID** (auto number or short code)
- **Date**
- **Decision** (one sentence)
- **Type** (scope / pillars / tech) *(optional but recommended)*
- **Decider**
- **Recommender** *(optional)*
- **Why (context)** (one sentence)

- **Trade-off / cost** (what we give up / what moves)
- **Impact** (scope/pillars/tech – short)
- **Links** (tickets/docs/build notes) *(if applicable)*
- **Revisit / reversal condition**
- **Status** (active / superseded) *(optional)*

A good decision log is scannable in under a minute.

Two rules that prevent paperwork rot

1) If it's not scannable, it won't be used.

Keep entries short. If a decision needs a novel to justify it, the work wasn't ready – or the team is trying to compensate for missing alignment.

2) If it doesn't change reality, it didn't happen.

When a decision affects committed work, it must be linked back to execution: backlog, one-pager, build notes, or whatever the team actually uses. "Links if applicable" is fine – but don't hide behind it when the link obviously exists.

How to extend later (only if it earns its keep)

If the team grows or the number of decisions increases, you can add:

- Tags (milestone, system, platform)
- Reversibility (easy to reverse vs hard to reverse)
- Impacted areas (QA, art, design)
- Communication status (announced / pending)

But don't start there. Start with Decision Cards or the minimal table, keep it alive for a month, and let real pain determine what you add.

VI. How to roll out templates without pushback: "start small," 1 team, 1 month, 1 area

Most template rollouts fail for predictable reasons. Not because templates are bad, but because teams smell "paperwork" and "process theater" from a mile away. If you roll it out as a big change, you'll get passive resistance: people nod, then keep deciding in DMs and shipping chaos as usual.

So treat rollout like production: small scope, clear exit criteria, short feedback loops. One team. One month. One area.

You chose **decision making** as the area. Good – because it's a leverage point. If decision flow improves, scope control and momentum improve downstream.

The framing that prevents "paperwork" backlash

Don't sell templates as documentation. Sell them as **a way to stop relitigating and reduce stress.**

The honest pitch is simple:

- "We're not adding process. We're removing repeated debates and DM decisions."
- "We'll run it with one team for one month."
- "If it doesn't pay back, we stop."

That "we can stop" clause matters. It makes the change safe.

Also: don't roll out four templates at once. That's where the "paperology" accusation becomes valid.

Pick the smallest viable starter set (for decision making)

For a one-month, one-team pilot in decision making, the minimum set that actually changes outcomes is:

1. **Decision Contract Starter** (roles + required inputs + escalation paths)
2. **Minimal Decision Log** (single table + one entry per decision)

3. **"Ready to Decide / Ready to Communicate" checklists** (as lightweight gates)

Notice what's not included: a full one-pager rewrite, elaborate pillars workshops, heavy meeting structures. Those can come later. For this pilot, you're proving one thing: decisions stop being fuzzy and start updating reality.

"1 team" selection: how to choose without politics

Pick a team that meets two criteria:

- they have enough dependency/complexity that decision pain is real (so the pilot matters),
- they have at least one lead who is not allergic to experiments (so it won't be sabotaged by cynicism).

Avoid the most dysfunctional team (too much fire to pilot) and avoid the happiest team (they don't feel the pain, so nobody cares). Pick the "normal struggling" team.

"1 month" plan (kept under 30 minutes per person per week)

This rollout only works if it's low-cost and high-signal. Your budget is 30 minutes per person per week, so you must keep it tight.

Week 0 (setup, producer-driven, mostly async):

- Publish a one-page Decision Contract Starter tailored to the team: who is decider for scope/pillars/tech in this team context, what inputs are required, and the two escalation paths. Keep it short.
- Create the Decision Log table and add 2–3 seed entries (recent decisions) to show what "good" looks like.
- Post the two checklists next to the log (same place, same visibility).

This week is mostly on you. Don't ask the team to "help design the process." That creates ownership theater and delays.

Weeks 1–4 (execution):

- Every decision that affects scope/pillars/tech must follow the contract and appear in the log. Not "eventually." Same day or next day.
- Use the "Ready to Decide" checklist as a pre-gate. If an item fails, you either fill missing inputs quickly or defer the decision. That alone eliminates a lot of wasted meetings.
- Use the "Ready to Communicate" checklist as a release gate. A decision isn't done until it's communicated with a link to a durable record. DM is allowed for discussion, not for final decisions.

Keep weekly touchpoints minimal. You don't need new meetings. You just need to enforce the gates when decisions happen anyway.

The key technique to avoid "this won't work here"

When someone says "this won't work in our project," they're usually reacting to two things:

- fear of overhead,
- fear that reality is messier than any template.

Don't argue. Use the pilot structure as the answer:

- "We're not standardizing the whole studio."
- "We're testing with one team for one month."
- "If it creates overhead without payoff, we kill it."

Then make it measurable and behavioral. Skepticism dies when people see fewer repeated debates and fewer surprise reversals.

What you do when pushback shows up (in practice)

Pushback: "This is paperwork."

Your response is not persuasion. It's subtraction. Ask: which field is noise? Remove it. The only fields that stay are the ones that prevent rework and rumor. The log entry should take minutes, not hours.

Pushback: "We don't have time."

Point out the swap: you're trading minutes of writing for hours of relitigating and rework. Then prove it by enforcing the stop-rule: no named decider, no decision. People quickly realize how much time was being wasted on "almost-decisions."

Pushback: "It won't work because decisions are messy."

Agree that decisions are messy. The contract doesn't make them clean. It makes them **visible and retrievable**. Messy but recorded beats messy and forgotten.

Success criteria after 1 month (proposed)

Concrete proposals. Here are simple criteria that map to outcomes, not vanity.

Behavioral success criteria:

- Fewer "surprise vetoes" and fewer "I thought we agreed" moments.
- Fewer decisions happening entirely in private messages.
- Clearer ownership: people can name who decides scope/pillars/tech without guessing.
- Less meeting churn: fewer repeat discussions on the same topic.

Operational success criteria (light KPI-based):

- Decision log has consistent entries for all scope/pillar/tech decisions in the month.
- Lead time on decisions decreases (fewer stuck items waiting for "someone").
- Interruption count drops (fewer priority flips caused by late decisions).
- Throughput/closure becomes more stable (because decisions stop reopening work).

Don't expect miracles in throughput in a month. Expect reduced churn and clearer execution. That's already a win.

Exit criteria (so this doesn't become process creep)

At the end of the month, you do a brutally simple review:

- What did we stop re-litigating?

- What became faster or calmer?
- What fields/rules were noise?
- Which parts should be dropped, kept, or expanded?

If the answer is "nothing improved," you stop. That's not failure – that's controlled experimentation. But in most teams, even a minimal decision log plus clear decider roles produces an immediate benefit: fewer ghost decisions, fewer reversals, less stress.

The producer's core job in this rollout

You don't "introduce templates." You enforce a single reality:

- decisions must be decision-ready,
- decisions must be recorded,
- decisions must be communicated in a durable way.

Start small, keep it cheap, prove payoff, and only then expand scope. That's how you roll out templates without triggering the immune system.

CHAPTER 7: Anonymized Case Files (alignment failures + recoveries)

I. Case 1: "The vision drifted between design and production" – symptoms, reset, outcome

They didn't lose the vision in one dramatic moment. They lost it the way most AA teams do: one "small improvement" at a time.

The project was in a healthy place on paper. A clear pitch, a solid prototype, a team that had shipped before. Production had a milestone plan. Design had a direction. Nobody felt like they were gambling.

Then the game entered the dangerous middle: enough progress to feel committed, not enough clarity to feel safe.

The drift: when "vision" becomes a moving target

It started innocently. A designer brought a feature idea that genuinely improved the experience – something that made the loop smoother, the feedback clearer, the player's choices more meaningful. It was the kind of change everyone wanted to say yes to.

It got discussed in chat. It got a few thumbs-up. Someone added a ticket "just to track it." A programmer picked it up because it looked small. It landed in a build. It was fun. That success became permission.

Soon, more "small improvements" followed. Each one was defensible in isolation. Each one was a local win. But nobody was holding the combined picture.

Production still talked in milestones. Design still talked in player experience. But the two maps stopped matching.

Every week, the backlog looked busier, and the game looked... different. Not worse. Different.

The team began to use a new sentence often: "We'll know when we play it."

That sentence is fine in early exploration. In mid-production, it's how vision becomes fog.

The hidden mechanism: no decider means no boundary

The core failure wasn't lack of talent or effort. It was structural: **there was no clear decider for scope packaging.**

Without a decider, "vision" drifts because every good idea feels equally valid, and every objection feels like personal taste. Decisions don't land as decisions. They land as momentum and pressure.

Design would push for improvements because the experience mattered. Production would accept them because the improvements seemed small and the team wanted quality. Tech would adapt because the changes were already in motion. QA would drown quietly because the surface area kept expanding.

No one was malicious. But the system rewarded feature creep.

The vision didn't drift because design changed its mind. It drifted because the project stopped having a hard boundary around what "wins" versus what "waits."

Symptoms: what people noticed before they admitted the problem

The symptoms arrived before the diagnosis. They always do.

First, it became harder to finish anything cleanly. Features were "almost done" forever because every improvement created a new edge case, new interaction, new tuning loop.

Second, estimates stopped meaning anything. Production could still track tasks, but not outcomes. Items moved on the board, yet the build didn't converge toward the milestone.

Third, priorities started conflicting in a way that felt personal. Designers felt production was blocking quality. Production felt design was ignoring reality. Tech felt caught between "do it fast" and "do it right." People started escalating in side conversations because there wasn't a clear decision path.

Fourth, the build became unstable – not always red, but unreliable enough that teams avoided touching certain systems. A fragile build is a psychological signal: it teaches the team to move carefully, which slows iteration, which increases pressure, which increases shortcuts.

And underneath all of that was the real symptom: trust in the plan faded. Not openly. Quietly. People stopped believing the milestone date. They kept working, but with less conviction.

The reset: scope cut as an act of alignment, not defeat

The turning point wasn't a clever planning session. It was a blunt realization: the game they were building was not the game they planned for – and the milestone was approaching whether they liked it or not.

The reset began with an uncomfortable question: "If we ship what we have now, what is the game?"

That question forced clarity. Not in a poetic way – in a packaging way. It forced someone to own the scope.

They didn't solve it by debate. They solved it by installing one missing piece: a **Project One-Pager** that became the single reference for what they were actually shipping.

This wasn't a big document. It was a hard boundary.

The one-pager had only what mattered:

- the win condition for the milestone,
- three pillars that described what "good" meant,
- constraints that were real (time, platform, build cadence),
- and – most importantly – explicit nongoals.

The nongoals were written like a shield, not a wish:

- "No new systems that expand the core loop."
- "No additional content categories."
- "No new progression layer."
- "No feature work that increases QA surface without removing something else."

Then came the scope cut.

Not a gentle "we'll prioritize." An actual cut: features were categorized as either necessary to deliver the promised experience, or not. Anything not necessary was moved out of the milestone packaging. Some work was reverted because it had expanded surface area without delivering a core win.

This is where many teams hesitate. They fear that cutting scope means lowering quality. In reality, it's the opposite: cutting scope is how you protect quality when the system is already overloaded.

The reset wasn't just deciding what to remove. It was deciding what would now be considered "done." Definition of done became strict: integrated, verified, no critical regressions, meets pillar intent. If it couldn't be verified in a reliable build, it wasn't done. If it wasn't done, it didn't count.

What changed after the reset (and why it worked)

Something subtle happened after the one-pager and the scope cut: conversations got shorter.

Not because people cared less. Because arguments had fewer degrees of freedom.

A designer could still propose improvements, but now the proposal had to answer: which pillar does this serve, and what do we trade for it? Without a trade, it wasn't a scope change – it was a wish.

Production could say no without politics, because "no" wasn't personal. It was anchored in the win condition and nongoals.

Tech stopped being the silent referee, because the packaging and trade-offs were explicit. QA stopped being the bearer of bad news, because the project stopped expanding its test surface every week.

And the backlog started matching reality again. Not perfectly, but enough that people could trust it.

They didn't become faster overnight. They became more predictable. Momentum returned because work could finally close.

Outcome: shipped, with corrected ambition

They shipped the milestone. Not the maximal version they originally imagined, but a version that was coherent and stable.

The game didn't feel like a compromised mess. It felt like a focused product. Some features were missing, yes. But the core loop was clear, the build was reliable, and the player experience stopped changing shape week to week.

Internally, the biggest win wasn't the shipped build. It was the restored agreement between design and production: design protected the experience by protecting pillars; production protected delivery by protecting boundaries; and scope changes stopped being informal.

The ambition wasn't killed. It was rescheduled – on purpose, instead of by accident.

That's the real lesson of this case: when vision drifts between design and production, it's rarely a creative problem. It's a packaging problem. And the fastest reset is not a bigger deck. It's a hard one-pager boundary plus a scope cut that makes the plan believable again.

II. Case 2: "Shadow leadership" – how to detect it, how to bring decisions into the open

It didn't look like a power grab.

It looked like efficiency.

The team was late, the backlog was noisy, and everyone was tired of meetings that ended with "we'll figure it out." In that environment, the person who can give a fast answer becomes a magnet. People start going to them not because they're trying to undermine leadership, but because they want the work to move.

That's how shadow leadership is born: not from ambition, but from a vacuum.

The setup: a team that stopped believing in formal decisions

This was an AA team, large enough that informal alignment didn't scale anymore. They had leads. They had a producer. They had planning. On paper, decisions had owners.

In reality, decisions were slow, soft, and reversible.

Design would propose a direction, production would "align," and then a week later the direction would shift again after another review, another chat, another strong opinion. People learned a pattern: formal decisions were not durable. They were suggestions.

So they adapted. Quietly.

Instead of waiting for a meeting, they started asking the person who gave reliable answers.

A charismatic designer – smart, articulate, quick – became that person. Not officially. But functionally.

At first it helped. Questions got answered. Work moved. The team felt less blocked.

Then the cost arrived.

The symptom: priorities that change, but nobody admits changing them

The producer began seeing strange signals:

Tasks would get deprioritized without a corresponding decision. A feature that was "locked for milestone" would suddenly get a new dependency. Something that was clearly not urgent would appear at the top of the board.

When asked, nobody could point to a clear decision moment. There wasn't one.

There were just... conversations.

The designer would have quick chats with different people. A suggestion would become a commitment. A commitment would become "everyone agreed." And because the person was persuasive and well-intentioned, nobody wanted to call it out as leadership.

It didn't feel like someone taking control. It felt like someone "helping."

But the producer noticed the pattern: different disciplines were now working from different versions of reality.

Engineering believed the priority was stability. Art believed the priority was new content. Design believed the priority was improving the loop. QA believed the priority was "whatever was broken today." Nobody was lying. They were all reacting to different inputs.

The backlog became a battlefield of silent edits.

How to detect shadow leadership without making it personal

Shadow leadership is not primarily about one person. It's about **decision channels.**

You can detect it by watching where decisions actually happen:

- People stop asking "who decides?" and start asking "who can I convince?"
- The real priority order lives in private threads, not in the plan.
- Changes show up first in implementation, not in decisions.
- Leads are surprised by work that started "somehow."
- The producer hears "I thought we agreed" more than "here is the recorded decision."

It also has a social signature: the shadow leader becomes the unofficial routing node. People ask them to unblock, to approve, to reinterpret what leadership "really wants." Over time, they become the translator between teams and formal leadership, which is a quiet form of power.

And the most dangerous part is that it often works – until it doesn't.

The damage: chaos in priorities, and a loss of trust in the system

Once shadow leadership takes root, the backlog stops being a plan. It becomes a ledger of arguments.

Priorities become unstable because decisions are not bound to a single decider and a single record. They're bound to persuasion and availability. Whoever had the last conversation wins.

This has three predictable outcomes:

First, throughput becomes erratic. Work starts, stops, restarts. Lead time grows. People become cautious, then heroic, then burned out.

Second, formal leads lose authority even when they're right. Not because the team disrespects them, but because the system taught the team that formal decisions don't stick.

Third, the shadow leader gets trapped too. They can't stop answering because the vacuum remains. They become overloaded, and their informal decisions become inconsistent, which increases chaos further.

It's a loop.

Eventually it hit an inflection point: a milestone review approached, and multiple "high priority" items were in flight that could not all be finished. Nobody could explain why those items were prioritized. The producer couldn't defend the plan because the plan had been rewritten socially.

That's when the studio paid the cost: a painful replan, dropped scope, and a week of pure friction.

Costly, but finally visible.

The intervention: bring decisions into the open with hard boundaries

They didn't fix it by asking everyone to "communicate better." That's a nice sentence that changes nothing.

They fixed it by changing the rules of what counts as a decision.

The producer drove a hard intervention with three moves.

Move 1: Define the decision channel and remove ambiguity

They introduced a minimal Decision Contract rule in plain language: discussion can happen anywhere, but decisions that affect scope, pillars, or tech direction must be recorded and announced. If it's not recorded, it's not real.

No drama. No blame. Just a new definition of reality.

Move 2: Install a visible decider for priority packaging

The project named one decider for scope and priority packaging. Not as a title, but as a functional role: when priorities conflict, this person makes the call. The producer made it explicit: everyone can contribute, but not everyone can steer.

This reduced the incentive to lobby privately, because lobbying no longer produced durable outcomes.

Move 3: Enforce the release gate ("ready to communicate")

A decision wasn't considered complete until it was communicated in a durable channel with a link to the decision record and the updated backlog. The producer stopped accepting "I told X" or "we discussed it" as communication.

The cost of this enforcement was social discomfort. People don't like having their informal influence limited, even when they intellectually agree. But the producer held the line because without enforcement, nothing changes.

How the shadow leader was handled (without humiliation)

The charismatic designer wasn't attacked. They were re-framed.

The producer had a direct conversation: the team is treating your opinions as decisions because the system is unclear. That's unfair to you and damaging to the project. We need you as a recommender and contributor, not an unofficial decider.

Then they gave the designer a legitimate channel: when they had a strong direction, they brought it as a decision-ready proposal with options, costs, risks, and pillar impact. Their influence didn't disappear. It became structured and visible.

That is the crucial distinction: the goal is not to remove influence. It's to remove invisible influence.

Outcome: costly, but repaired – and calmer

The project didn't avoid pain. The week of replanning happened. Some scope was cut. Some work was reclassified as "nice-to-have" and deferred. People were annoyed. That's normal when you surface reality after weeks of soft decisions.

But after the reset, something improved quickly: priorities stopped changing invisibly.

When a priority changed, it was now attached to a decision record and a trade-off. People could disagree, but they couldn't pretend the change didn't have a cost. The backlog became trustworthy again.

Shadow leadership faded not because someone lost charisma, but because the team stopped needing an unofficial decision channel to move.

That's the real lesson of the case:

Shadow leadership is not a personality problem. It's a systems problem.
You detect it by watching where decisions really happen.
You fix it by making the decision channel explicit, naming deciders, and enforcing a release gate that turns decisions into shared reality.

III. Case 3: "We changed scope every week" – change control without bureaucracy

Every Monday looked the same.

A fresh list of "must-have" changes arrived from above – sometimes from a stakeholder call, sometimes from a forwarded message that began with: "Quick thought." Each change sounded reasonable. Most of them were even good. The problem wasn't the ideas.

The problem was the rhythm: the project changed scope every week, and nobody was paying the true cost.

This was an AA project in mid-production, far enough along that the team had real content and systems, but not close enough to lock the finish line. The stakeholders were engaged and opinionated. They cared. They also created pressure by treating the game as something that could be steered continuously without friction.

The team tried to be responsive. That's how it slipped into chaos.

The weekly pattern: a project that never settles

At first, changes were handled like "normal agile." People would adjust. The producer would update priorities. The team would scramble. And somehow the week would end with something shipped in the build.

Then a subtle shift happened: work stopped finishing and started *circulating*.

A feature would be half-implemented, then paused because a new "urgent" change came in. The next week it would be reopened, but now it no longer matched the latest direction. So it required rework. Meanwhile, two other areas were now also half-done, each carrying its own set of assumptions.

The backlog grew, but not in a clean way. It grew in the middle: WIP, "almost done," "needs polish," "blocked by decision," "waiting for feedback." The team had motion, not momentum.

Stakeholders didn't see the accumulating cost. They saw responsiveness. And responsiveness became the expectation.

What the producer could see (even if nobody said it out loud)

The symptoms weren't dramatic. They were corrosive:

- Plans stopped being trusted. The team stopped treating sprint goals as real, because they had learned they could be overwritten.
- People started hedging: implementing flexible systems "just in case" to survive the next change.
- QA became a bottleneck and a scapegoat: every week changed what had to be tested.
- Lead time grew quietly. Throughput became unpredictable. Builds became shakier because integration was happening under constant churn.

The emotional signal was even clearer: the team started asking, "What's the point of finishing this if it'll change next week?"

That's the moment you lose a project – not in schedule, but in spirit.

The false solutions they tried first

They tried to "communicate better." More syncs. Longer notes. More alignment calls. None of it helped because the mechanism didn't change.

They also tried to "push back harder." That created conflict and politics, because the pushback was personal: producer vs stakeholder, team vs leadership. It wasn't anchored in a fair system.

They were stuck between two bad modes:

- accept changes and drown,
- or fight changes and burn relationships.

What they were missing was a third mode: **accept change, but only through a controlled gate** that makes cost visible and forces trade-offs – without bureaucracy.

The minimal fix: Evaluate -> Decide -> Communicate (and nothing else)

The turnaround started when the producer reframed the goal: not "stop changes," but "stop invisible changes."

They introduced one rule that everyone could understand:

Any change that affects scope must go through: Evaluate -> Decide -> Communicate.

Not a committee. Not a workflow diagram. A gate.

And the gate was intentionally lightweight.

Evaluate: What does this change cost, what does it break, what does it displace?
Decide: Do we accept it, reject it, or trade it for something else? Who owns that call?
Communicate: Update reality so the whole team works from the same plan.

The producer didn't require forms. They required three things to be stated in plain language:

- the change request,
- the impact (time/risk/what it displaces),
- and the trade-off decision.

The stakeholder could still request anything. The team would still respond. But now every request had to pass through a cost lens before it could become work.

That single change did two important things:

1. it shifted the conversation from "Do we like this?" to "What do we trade for this?"
2. it made "yes" meaningful again, because it came with explicit displacement.

Why it still didn't save them (and what the case teaches)

The system worked – when it was used.

But mid-production pressure has a predictable failure mode: people start bypassing the gate "just this once." And once bypassing works, it spreads.

Stakeholders would still message individuals directly. A lead would think, "I can squeeze it in." A designer would want to please. A programmer would try to be helpful. Small changes would slip into the build before the producer even saw them.

The team started doing Evaluate -> Decide -> Communicate *sometimes*. And "sometimes" is not a rule. It's a suggestion.

Because enforcement was inconsistent, the same weekly churn continued. The project did ship a lot of what was asked for – by paying with the two resources stakeholders rarely see until it's too late: **quality and people.**

Bugs increased. Polish slipped. Rework piled up. Overtime crept in, then became normal. The team kept "making it work," but the cost was compounding.

By the time leadership noticed the burnout signals and quality drift, the team had already spent months in survival mode.

They delivered. But they delivered a version of the game that was more fragile than it needed to be, and a team that needed recovery.

What "change control without bureaucracy" actually means

This case shows the hard truth: the minimal gate is enough, but only if it is real.

Change control without bureaucracy isn't "no process." It's **one enforceable rule** that keeps change from becoming stealth work:

- Evaluate makes cost visible,
- Decide forces trade-offs,
- Communicate prevents rumor-driven execution.

If you don't enforce it consistently, your project becomes a weekly rewrite. If you do enforce it, stakeholders can still influence direction – but they can't do it for free.

And that's the real purpose of change control: not to block change, but to stop pretending change is cheap.

IV. Case 4: "Platform/perf crisis" – bringing constraints into alignment

They thought they were late. Then they learned they were wrong about *what they were late on*.

The milestone was approaching. The feature list looked "mostly there." The build worked well enough on developer machines. The team's conversations were about polish and bug cleanup – the normal late-production soundtrack.

Then console performance and stability stopped being a "tech topic" and became the project.

Not with a slow warning. With a hard wall.

The moment the crisis becomes real

The first sign was familiar: a build that "sometimes" crashed on the target platform, but not reliably enough to debug quickly. The second sign was worse: even when it didn't crash, the frame pacing was inconsistent. Not a constant low frame rate – something more insidious. It felt unstable.

Players notice that kind of instability instantly. Even non-technical stakeholders feel it in their hands.

The producer watched a late build run on the platform and saw the room shift. Nobody said "we're in trouble," but everyone moved like they heard it.

The team reacted the way teams often do:

- engineering tried to fix stability fast,
- design tried to preserve experience,
- art tried to protect visual identity,
- production tried to protect the milestone date.

All reasonable instincts. All incompatible without a shared constraint truth.

Why it happened: the constraints were never aligned

This crisis wasn't caused by one bad optimization choice. It was caused by a missing shared constraint.

Everyone "knew" performance mattered. But they didn't share a concrete, enforced definition of what performance stability meant for this platform and this phase.

So the project evolved with invisible assumptions:

- features were approved without considering platform cost,
- content was added without a clear runtime budget,
- and stability work competed with everything else because it looked like "tech debt," not delivery risk.

Late production punishes that kind of ambiguity. The cost compounds until it becomes unavoidable.

The real conflict wasn't engineering vs design. It was **constraints vs wishes.**

Symptoms: when constraints are ignored, the project tells on itself

Before the crisis, the warning signals were already there, but they were interpreted as "normal late pressure":

- bug counts rising without clear closure,
- build confidence dropping ("don't touch that system right now"),
- more "it works on my machine" moments,
- and regression fear driving slower iteration.

Those are not just technical problems. They are alignment problems. They indicate that the project no longer has a shared "what wins" rule when time is tight.

The reset: constraints become the central pillar of the milestone

The producer didn't start the reset with a performance lecture. They started with a packaging lecture.
They gathered leads and made one statement that shifted the project:

For this platform and this phase, stability is not a technical concern. It is the product.

That line reframed every decision. If stability is the product, then anything that harms stability is not "nice-to-have polish." It's scope that threatens shipping.

Then they did something crucial: they brought constraints into alignment by writing them down in a place everyone already recognized as authoritative – the project's one-page alignment artifact. Not a separate performance wiki nobody reads. A constraint block that sat next to pillars and scope.

The constraint was stated plainly:

- "Target platform build must be stable enough for continuous testing."
- "Frame pacing must be consistent enough to meet the platform's experience expectation."
- "Any change that risks stability is automatically treated as high risk and must go through a decision gate."

No fancy numbers were required in the narrative. The point was to make the constraint explicit, shared, and enforceable.

The mechanism: Evaluate -> Decide -> Communicate, now applied to performance

At this point, teams often fall into chaos: "all hands optimize," "stop all features," "panic mode." That can work for a week. It can also destroy the project's coherence.

Instead, they used the minimal change pipeline they already had:

Evaluate -> Decide -> Communicate.

Every change request – especially last-minute polish – had to answer:

- does it improve or risk stability?
- what does it cost?
- what does it displace?
- what is the rollback plan if it harms stability?

This is how you prevent performance work from becoming a black hole: you keep decisions explicit and tied to trade-offs.

The hard part: choosing a downgrade on purpose

As stability work progressed, they hit the uncomfortable truth: they could not keep full visual ambition and hit stability on the target platform in time.

This is where projects either die in denial or survive through an intentional downgrade.

They chose intentional.

The downgrade wasn't a vague "lower quality." It was a controlled set of cuts tied to the constraint:

- reduce heavy runtime features that created unpredictable spikes,
- simplify effects that were destabilizing frame pacing,
- reduce content complexity in the worst offender scenarios,
- and remove edge-case behaviors that caused rare but brutal crashes.

These decisions hurt artistically. They also saved the product.

The key was that the downgrade was framed as a trade-off decision, not as defeat:

- "We are choosing stability over fidelity for this platform in this milestone."
- "We will protect the core experience and ship a consistent game."
- "We will revisit higher fidelity only if stability remains green and we have runway."

That last line matters. It keeps morale intact. It acknowledges ambition without pretending you can afford it today.

Outcome: stability achieved, quality adjusted, trust restored

They shipped a stable console build. It wasn't the most visually impressive version of the game. But it was playable, consistent, and defensible.

More importantly, the team regained trust in the plan because the plan matched the reality of constraints. People stopped improvising priorities and started finishing again.

The crisis also taught the project a durable rule:

If constraints are not explicit, the project will pick them for you – late, painfully, and without your consent.

What "bringing constraints into alignment" really means

It's not a document exercise. It's a decision exercise.

Bringing constraints into alignment means:

- the team shares the same hard limits,
- those limits are written where decisions are made (not hidden in tech lore),
- and the change pipeline treats constraint-risk as first-class.

In late production, that's often the difference between "we keep trying to polish" and "we actually ship."

V. Case 5: "The team stopped believing dates" – rebuilding trust in the plan

Nobody announced it. There was no dramatic meeting where someone said, "We don't believe the schedule anymore."

It happened quietly, the way trust usually dies in production: in small, repeated disappointments.

The dates were still on the roadmap. The milestones were still on the wall. The producer still sent updates. Leads still attended planning. Everything looked normal.

And yet the team had stopped *acting* like dates were real.

The erosion: when the plan becomes background noise

At first the signs were subtle.

People would nod at sprint goals and then work in a way that didn't converge. Tasks stayed "in progress" longer than expected. Items rolled over. The team kept shipping *something*, but the closure rate never matched the plan.

Then the language shifted.

Instead of "we'll finish it by Friday," it became "we'll see how far we get." Instead of "we're on track," it became "we're not blocked, but..." People stopped making commitments in public. They started protecting themselves.

That's a morale problem, but it's also a system problem. When a team learns that commitments are punished by reality, they stop committing.

The producer could feel it in meetings: less energy, more defensive phrasing, fewer optimistic plans. Not because people didn't care. Because caring had become exhausting.

The cause: chronic underestimation turns dates into lies

This wasn't a "scope creep every week" story. It was more insidious: the scope was relatively stable, but **estimates were consistently wrong.**

Not by a little. By enough that every plan was a polite fiction.

The team was estimating implementation effort, not completion effort. They were underestimating integration, verification, iteration, and the hidden work that turns "done in code" into "done in the build."

They also underestimated uncertainty. Early unknowns were treated like known work. Risk wasn't priced in. Dependencies were assumed away. "We'll handle it when we get there" became the default.

And because underestimation was chronic, the schedule didn't serve the team anymore. It served only as a reporting artifact.

That's the moment dates lose meaning: when they stop being a tool for coordination and start being a story for stakeholders.

The daily impact: morale drops without obvious conflict

When teams don't believe dates, you don't always see rebellion. You see resignation.

People stop pushing for clarity, because clarity doesn't seem to change outcomes. They stop raising risks early, because risks are always "handled later." They stop treating planning as a serious act, because planning has become theatre.

The project becomes heavier. Not because work increased, but because the emotional load increased: every plan feels like setting yourself up for failure.

That's how chronic underestimation damages morale. It teaches people that truth is unsafe.

The reset: rebuild trust using flow, not promises

The producer didn't fix this by demanding "better estimates." That's the classic mistake.

Better estimates don't happen because you ask for them. They happen because you change the system so estimates are anchored in reality.

The reset started with a hard decision: stop forecasting based on hope, and start forecasting based on observed flow.

They introduced a simple, project-level baseline:

- **Throughput** (real "done" items per week),
- **Lead time** (typical start-to-done),
- **Build stability** (can we reliably verify work).

Not as a dashboard for leadership. As a mirror for the team.

The producer framed it bluntly and calmly: "We won't win trust by promising dates. We'll win it by shipping predictably."

Then they did the part most teams avoid: they reduced scope to match reality.

Scope cut: the painful step that makes the plan believable

Once the team had a few weeks of throughput and lead time data, the mismatch became undeniable. The plan required a closure rate the project wasn't producing.

That's where you either lie louder or you cut scope.

They cut scope.

Not randomly. They cut based on the simplest rule: protect what makes the game coherent, remove what multiplies uncertainty.

They focused on:

- removing features that were still ambiguous or high-iteration,
- reducing content volume that expanded QA surface,
- deferring anything that added integration risk late,
- and tightening "definition of done" so closure was real.

The scope cut wasn't presented as defeat. It was presented as reclaiming reality: "We can ship a coherent version with high confidence, or we can keep pretending we'll ship everything and burn out."

That honesty is what teams respond to. Not optimism.

How trust was rebuilt, step by step

The trust didn't return because someone made a speech. It returned because the plan started matching lived experience.

Small but important shifts happened:

First, planning became shorter and more conservative – based on **what actually closes**, not what theoretically could be done. People started making commitments again because commitments were survivable.

Second, the producer protected closure. They reduced WIP, pushed for small finishes, and treated build stability as a priority. This increased the rate of real "done," which is the only currency that buys credibility.

Third, dates became fewer and firmer. Instead of big promises, the team used short horizons where flow was visible. The roadmap stopped being a fantasy novel and became a sequence of achievable closures.

Morale improved not because the project became easy, but because it became honest.

Outcome: fewer features, stronger plan, calmer team

They shipped a smaller game than originally imagined. But they shipped a game that was predictable to build and stable to test.

The team didn't become "happy" overnight. But the cynicism faded. People stopped treating dates as a joke because dates stopped behaving like a joke.

And the producer gained something more valuable than a bigger scope: a team that believed the plan again.

The lesson

When a team stops believing dates, don't ask for faith. Don't demand better estimation. Don't pressure people into optimism.

Do three things:

- measure flow (throughput, lead time, build stability),
- plan based on reality,
- and cut scope until the plan becomes believable.

Trust is rebuilt when the plan stops lying.

VI. Case template: context -> signals -> mistake -> intervention -> cost -> lesson -> artifact

This template is for a producer's internal use. Its job is to turn "we had a mess" into a **repeatable rule + a concrete artifact**. It forces clarity and numbers. If you can't fill a field, that's also a signal (you didn't have the instrumentation, the definition of done, or a stable decision trail).
Use it as a one-page entry in Notion/Confluence/Google Docs.

Producer Case Template (one page)

Title (one line):

Short, neutral name (e.g., "Weekly scope churn from stakeholder pressure").

1) Context (what, when, constraints)

- Team size + structure (e.g., AA, 35 people, 4 leads)
- Phase (pre / mid / late)
- Hard constraints (platform, milestone, budget/runway)
- What "success" meant *at that time* (one sentence)

2) Signals (early warnings) (must include numbers)

List 3–6 signals. Each signal must have a **metric** and (ideally) a trend.

Pick metrics that fit your project:

- Throughput: ______ "done" items/week (trend)
- Lead time (median): ______ days (trend)
- WIP: ______ items in progress (trend)
- Interruptions: ______ priority flips/week
- Build stability: ______ green-build days/week, ______ blockers/week
- Reopen rate: ______ % items reopened from QA
- Overtime: ______ hours/person/week (if tracked)
- Crash rate (platform): ______ per session/hour (if relevant)

3) Mistake (one root mistake, not a list)

One sentence. Use this format:
"We allowed **X** without **Y**, so **Z** happened."
(Example: "We allowed scope changes without explicit trade-offs, so the backlog stopped being trustworthy.")

4) Intervention (what changed, in what order)

3–5 steps, each with a horizon:

- Step 1 (48h): ______
- Step 2 (2 weeks): ______
- Step 3 (1 month): ______

5) Cost (what we paid) *(must include numbers)*

- Scope cut: ______ features / ______ % content deferred
- Schedule impact: ______ days/weeks slip OR "no slip, but cut"
- Quality impact: ______ (e.g., downgrade areas, bug count trend)
- People impact: ______ (overtime peak, churn risk signals)
- Opportunity cost: ______ (what we stopped doing)

6) Lesson (transferable rule)

1–2 sentences in rule form:
"If **[condition]**, then **[rule]**, because **[reason]**."

7) Artifact (what we created/updated to prevent recurrence)

Choose one (or "None" with a reason):

- One-pager update (pillars/constraints/nongoals)
- Decision contract / decision log / ready-checklists
- Change gate (Evaluate -> Decide -> Communicate)
- Definition of Done update
- **None** (one sentence why)

8) Optional: Anti-lesson (what NOT to do next time)

1–2 short bullets: actions that felt productive but made things worse.

Mini example fill (compressed)

Title: Weekly scope churn from stakeholder pressure

1) Context: AA team, 42 people, mid-production. Hard constraint: external review every 2 weeks. Success = stable milestone slice with predictable closure.

2) Signals (numbers): Throughput dropped 18 -> 9 done/week (3 weeks). Median lead time rose 6 -> 14 days. WIP grew 22 -> 41. Interruptions: 7 priority flips/week. Green-build days: 5 -> 2/week.

3) Mistake: We allowed scope changes without explicit trade-offs, so priorities became rumor-driven and work stopped closing.

4) Intervention: (48h) Freeze new scope intake; force closure on top 5 items with strict DoD. (2 weeks) Enforce Evaluate->Decide->Communicate for any scope change; require a trade-off. (1 month) Tighten milestone packaging, reduce WIP permanently, link decisions to backlog.

5) Cost: Deferred 6 features (~15% scope). No date slip, but polish reduced in two areas. Overtime peaked at ~6h/person/week for 2 weeks.

6) Lesson: If scope changes are socially cheap, they become operationally expensive. Every "yes" must include a visible "instead."

7) Artifact: Change gate checklist + decision log entries linked from the backlog.

8) Anti-lesson (optional): Don't "communicate harder" instead of changing the decision channel. Don't treat DM approvals as real decisions.

CHAPTER 8:
Console AddOn

I. Design/UX implications (what consoles change)

When you port an action game from PC to consoles, you're not "just changing controls." You're moving the game into a different living room ecosystem with different habits, tolerance thresholds, and failure modes.

PC players will forgive friction if the game is deep and modifiable. Console players will tolerate far less. Not because they're picky. Because the console experience is designed around one promise: **press a button, it works, it feels good, and it doesn't fight you.**

That promise has consequences for design and UX. Here are the ones that actually matter.

Input/controller: mapping, comfort, remap, dead zones

On PC, players bring their own input philosophy. Some are keyboard purists. Some play on controller. Some rebind everything. The hardware is messy, so expectations are flexible.

On console, the controller is the primary interface, and it's standardized. That changes what "good" feels like.

Mapping is not just functional. It's muscle memory.

If you ship a layout that fights the platform's dominant conventions, your game will feel "off" in the first five minutes. Players might not articulate why. They'll just feel friction. And friction in action games is lethal because it shows up as missed dodges, wrong inputs, and "the game didn't listen."

So the porting mindset should be: start with platform-native conventions and deviate only when you have a strong reason. Then teach the deviation clearly.

Comfort is part of design, not a nice-to-have.

A keyboard player can adjust posture easily. A controller player will do thousands of micro-movements with thumbs and triggers. A bad input scheme creates fatigue. Fatigue turns into sloppy play. Sloppy play turns into frustration. That's not "player skill." That's UX debt.

Common comfort traps in action ports:

- too many important actions on face buttons without sensible prioritization,
- sprint/hold actions that clash with camera control,
- awkward chord combos (press-and-hold + face button + stick click) used as "shortcuts."

Remapping is strongly recommended, and on action games it's a trust signal.

Even a basic remap system tells players: "we respect your hands." It also reduces support issues because players can solve their own comfort problems. If full remapping is too heavy, ship at least:

- multiple presets,
- invert axis,
- sensitivity options,
- and separate aim/look tuning where relevant.

Dead zones are the hidden reason players call your game 'floaty.'

If dead zones and response curves are wrong, your input will feel imprecise even if your game logic is correct. Console players will blame the game instantly. Don't treat dead zones as a technical checkbox. They define the "feel" of your movement and aim. For action games, that is core design.

The practical rule: if combat relies on precision, you need tuning that doesn't force one "feel" on everyone. A few basic options go a long way.

UI: safe areas, couch readability, focus, navigation

PC UI often assumes a player is 60 cm from the screen with a mouse. Console UI assumes a player is several meters away on a TV, with a controller, and a varied mix of screen sizes and overscan weirdness.

That changes everything.

Safe areas are not optional.

If important UI elements are near the edges, some players literally won't see them. That's not a "rare bug." It's a real-world setup issue you have to design for. When your UI gets cropped, the player doesn't blame their TV settings. They blame your game.

Couch readability is brutal.

Action games need fast comprehension. If a player squints at the HUD or can't parse menus quickly, they lose flow. And on console, losing flow often means quitting for the night.

Design implications:

- prefer fewer, larger, clearer elements over dense information layouts,
- avoid thin fonts and low-contrast styles,
- don't rely on hover states or tiny tooltips as primary explanation.

Focus and navigation are a different paradigm.

On PC, you can allow messy UI because the mouse can reach anything instantly. On console, you need a coherent focus path. "Where am I?" must always be obvious. Getting lost in menu focus is one of the fastest ways to destroy the "premium console" feel.

The simplest rule: every menu screen should be navigable with a predictable pattern, without hunting. If your UI has dozens of small interactive elements, you either redesign it or you accept constant friction.

Don't punish players with slow menus.

On console, players expect menus to respond immediately. This is not a luxury expectation. It's baseline. If there's input lag, stutter, or long transitions, they will feel the game is unstable – even if gameplay is fine.

Player expectations: stability, speed, "zero jank" in menus

Console players have a shorter patience window for jank, especially outside gameplay.

They might accept occasional chaos in a chaotic action scene. They will not accept jank in:

- menus,
- inventory,
- settings,
- loadouts,
- and screen transitions.

This is where ports often fail emotionally. The team focuses on frame rate in gameplay, but ships a menu system that hitches, stalls, or drops inputs. Players read that as "this port is sloppy."

So treat menus as part of the first impression, not as secondary polish.

A hard standard that helps: **menus must feel stable even when gameplay is heavy.** If opening the menu stutters because the game is streaming, allocating memory, or building UI dynamically, you've made the UI a performance victim. Console players will not separate those concerns. They'll just feel "this is janky."

Performance as part of design: trade-offs in VFX, crowds, simulation

In action games, performance isn't just a technical metric. It shapes the player's perception of control, responsiveness, and fairness.

On PC, you can partially externalize performance problems to settings. On console, you can't. You ship one experience. That makes performance a design constraint.

Every big VFX moment is a design choice.

On console, heavy VFX can steal clarity and stability at the same time. When effects cause hitching or drop responsiveness, players don't think "GPU." They think "the game cheated." The input felt late. The dodge didn't register. The parry window felt inconsistent.

That's a design failure.

So VFX trade-offs aren't just "lower quality." They're:

- keep clarity under pressure,
- keep control consistent,
- keep feedback readable.

Crowds and simulation are seductive and expensive.

PC versions often ship with richer simulation density because the high-end machine absorbs it. Console ports expose the reality: those systems cost stability. The design implication is blunt: if a feature creates instability, it's not "a cool extra." It's a threat to the core loop.

The mature move is to define what the experience needs, then cap the rest:

- cap crowd counts,
- cap AI complexity per scene,
- cap physics interactions that don't change gameplay outcomes.

This is where teams get stuck emotionally because they fear "downgrading." The healthier framing is: **we're protecting the feel of the game.** Action games live and die on feel.

Consistency beats peak spectacle.

Console players will forgive slightly less spectacle if the game is stable and responsive. They will not forgive a port that sometimes feels great and sometimes feels broken. That variability reads as low quality.

The practical takeaway for a PC-to-console action port

You don't win console UX by copying your PC UX and patching around it. You win by accepting four realities:

- controller feel is design,
- focus navigation is a first-class UI problem,
- zero-jank menus are a baseline expectation,
- and performance constraints must shape what you ship, not just how you optimize.

If you internalize those constraints early, the port becomes a controlled adaptation. If you ignore them, the port becomes an endless fight between "what we built" and "what consoles tolerate."

II. Build/Production implications (pipeline/builds/submission cadence)

When you ship on PC and consoles in parallel, the biggest trap is assuming the console pipeline behaves like PC with extra steps. It doesn't. Console shipping changes the physics of your production: builds aren't "cheap," submission introduces latency, and stability work becomes a schedule driver.

But the most common operational failure isn't even submission. It's what happens **before** submission: branching, stabilization, and the team's ability to freeze without collapsing into panic hotfix mode.

This subchapter is about that reality – how to keep your pipeline sane when you're running PC live and feeding console builds in the background.

Build cadence: PC vs console, and the cost of "every attempt"

On PC, you can get away with high-frequency iteration. Builds can be pushed quickly, distribution is flexible, and when you make a mistake you can often recover without a long external delay. That freedom trains teams into a habit: "just try it."

On consoles, "just try it" is expensive. Even before you hit first-party submission, you pay in:

- longer build times and packaging steps,
- environment setup differences,
- heavier QA verification (because the build is less disposable),
- and slower feedback loops when you need to test on target hardware.

The dangerous misunderstanding is not that console builds are slower. It's that console builds create a **queue**. If you treat them like PC builds (constant churn), you generate a backlog of verification work that your QA and engineers cannot absorb.

This is why build cadence is not a technical detail. It's a production policy.

A healthy approach is to define what "normal" means:

- PC can tolerate frequent updates and experimentation.
- Console needs fewer, more intentional drops – each one worth verifying.

If you don't set that expectation, the team will attempt console builds too often, and every attempt will steal time from actual delivery.

Branching and stabilization for cert: when to freeze, when to hotfix

When cert approaches, your pipeline must shift from "feature throughput" to "risk reduction." That shift is where teams fall apart, especially if they've been running one branch culture the whole time.

The core question is simple: **where does stabilization happen, and how do you protect it from churn?**

Below are two common strategies. Neither is perfect. The point is to choose one deliberately and accept its trade-offs.

Strategy A: "Main + Release branch" (classic stabilization)

- **Main** continues active development (PC live work, features, ongoing changes).
- **Release** is cut for console stabilization and stays protected.
- Only vetted, intentionally selected changes are cherry-picked into Release.

Why it works:

- Stabilization becomes a protected activity, not something that competes with daily churn.
- QA can test Release without it changing under their feet.
- You can keep PC moving while console stabilizes.

The cost:

- Cherry-picking becomes a discipline and a skill. If your codebase isn't modular or your team isn't used to it, you'll create conflicts and mistakes.

- People will try to "sneak" changes into Release because they feel urgent.
- You need clear decision rights: who approves what enters Release.

When it fails:

- When the Release branch becomes a dumping ground ("just put it there"), you lose the whole point.
- When Main diverges wildly and you end up re-solving the same issues twice.

A simple rule that protects this strategy: **Release is boring by design.** If it's exciting, you're doing it wrong.

Strategy B: "Stabilize on Main" (single-trunk discipline)

- You keep one mainline branch and stabilize directly there.
- Feature intake slows or stops_toggle; changes are tightly controlled for everyone.
- Hotfixes and cert prep are done without cutting a separate Release branch.

Why it works:

- No merge/cherry-pick complexity. One reality.
- Everyone sees the true state of the product, and nobody hides behind "it's only on Main."
- If your team has strong discipline, this can be clean and fast.

The cost:

- Your whole studio's velocity drops during stabilization.
- If you have live PC obligations, you must be extremely careful not to let PC urgency destabilize cert readiness.
- Any mistake hits everyone immediately.

When it fails:

- When the org can't say "no" to new work, stabilization on Main becomes perpetual whiplash.
- When urgent PC issues keep forcing changes and you never get a stable baseline long enough to validate.

If you're running PC live in parallel, Strategy B is high risk unless you already have a culture of "freeze means freeze."

Freeze and hotfix: what teams get wrong

The most common misunderstanding is treating "freeze" as a calendar event. "We freeze on Friday." Then Friday arrives, and the team is still in flux. Freeze becomes symbolic.

A real freeze is a **behavior change**:

- scope intake changes (you stop pulling new work),
- change evaluation becomes stricter,
- and the threshold for "this goes in" gets higher.

Hotfixes are where teams rationalize breaking the freeze. They say "it's just a small fix." Then they ship a small fix that touches a risky area, destabilizes another system, and now they need another hotfix. That spiral kills cert timelines.

The practical principle is: **hotfix is not a type of work, it's a type of risk.** If you hotfix without a gate, you're not protecting schedule – you're gambling with it.

The healthier approach is to treat freeze like a risk budget:

- If you change something during freeze, you spend risk budget.
- If risk budget runs out, you stop changing anything unless it's truly blocking submission.

This is also where producers need backbone. Freeze without enforcement is just a polite suggestion.

Submission reality: buffers, windows, first-party dependencies

Even if you don't go into the details of specific requirements, you must design around one reality: first-party submission is a dependency chain you don't control.

There are windows, reviews, processing time, potential back-and-forth, and external constraints that can affect when you can actually ship. The documentation and requirements are rigorous for a reason: platform holders care about user experience, stability, compliance, and ecosystem integrity.

Two production implications matter most:

1. **Buffers are not pessimism.** They are acknowledging latency and uncertainty you cannot eliminate.
2. **Your "ready" date is not your "release" date.** There is a gap, and it's not optional.

Teams that ignore this gap end up "done" at the last moment and then get surprised by the reality of submission timing.

How to plan team work when builds aren't cheap

This is the operational heart of it: if console builds and cert verification cost real time, you can't run the team as if every iteration is free.

The key planning shift is to separate work into two flows:

- **PC live flow** (fast iteration, frequent changes, more tolerance for churn),
- **Console stabilization flow** (intentional changes, lower frequency, higher verification burden).

Then you protect stabilization flow from PC urgency by policy, not hope.

In practice, that means:

- You decide which changes are allowed into the console stabilization stream.
- You limit how often you "drop" console builds so QA can actually validate them.
- You avoid pulling in new scope late, even if it looks small, because late scope is never just scope – it's verification cost.

If you want one sentence to anchor the whole subchapter, it's this:

On consoles, the cost of every attempt is real. If you don't control attempts, attempts will control your schedule.

That's the difference between a port that feels like production and a port that feels like endless triage.

III. Risk triggers checklist (when to treat as risk + buffer rules)

Console risk management fails in one predictable way: teams treat risky changes like normal changes until the platform punishes them. By the time the punishment arrives (instability, regressions, submission delays), the schedule is already spent.

So this checklist is intentionally conservative. It's designed for late-stage console realities where builds aren't cheap, verification takes time, and "we'll know tomorrow" is not a valid plan.

The goal is not to be afraid of change. The goal is to **classify it correctly** and apply buffers before you're forced to.

Core rule: "risk" means "extra verification + extra latency"

On PC, risky changes can be corrected quickly. On console, risky changes cost you twice: they create regressions *and* they extend the time before you can confidently ship the next candidate. That's why risk triggers must be explicit.

Risk Triggers Checklist (Trigger -> Consequence -> Action)

A) Gameplay-critical and platform-sensitive changes

Trigger: Saves / persistence (formats, serialization, versioning, migration)

- **Consequence:** invisible breakage, corrupted progression, hard-to-repro issues, late discovery.
- **Action:** treat as high risk. Require "Ready to Decide" inputs + explicit rollback plan + compatibility verification. Add buffer rules (below). Escalate sign-off.

Trigger: Input (mapping, remap, dead zones, input buffering, controller-specific behavior)

- **Consequence:** feel regressions, accessibility complaints, certification risk if input flows break expectations.

- **Action:** treat as risk. Require cross-discipline review (design + QA + tech). Communicate to everyone impacted (UI, tutorial, settings). Add buffer.

Trigger: UI flow / navigation / focus model

- **Consequence:** "zero jank" failures in menus, soft-locks, broken flow, platform UX expectation violations.
- **Action:** treat as risk. Require targeted console UX pass + regression checklist run. Add buffer.

Trigger: Performance/stability (frame pacing, streaming, memory, crash fixes that touch broad systems)

- **Consequence:** "fix one crash, create three new ones," unstable builds, inability to validate.
- **Action:** treat as risk by default. Require change gating + verification window + decision record. Add buffer. Consider freeze discipline (don't churn).

Trigger: Online systems (auth, matchmaking, network state, entitlements, DLC checks)

- **Consequence:** platform account edge cases, compliance failures, unpredictable QA surface.
- **Action:** treat as high risk. Require explicit test matrix and sign-off. Add buffer.

Trigger: SDK / platform integrations (trophies/achievements, user profiles, storage, telemetry hooks, storefront interactions)

- **Consequence:** first-party dependency issues, compliance failures, resubmissions.
- **Action:** treat as high risk. Require decision-ready inputs and sign-off; avoid late churn unless blocking.

B) Packaging and content pipeline changes

Trigger: Changes to content pipeline that affect packaging

(examples: asset bundle rules, compression, chunking, build scripts, localization pipeline, DLC packaging, patch packaging rules)

- **Consequence:** "build works locally, breaks in packaging," install/patch issues, unexpected size, broken loads, submission surprises.
- **Action:** treat as high risk. Require a verification build drop and full packaging validation. Add buffer. Escalate sign-off if it touches release candidate flow.

Simple Buffer Rules (conservative defaults)

These are not "schedule padding." They're a recognition that risky console changes expand verification time and reduce your ability to attempt again quickly.

When to add +1 week

Add **+1 week** when the change touches **one** high-risk area and is reasonably contained:

- UI flow changes limited to a few screens
- input mapping/options changes without deep systemic impact
- performance tuning that doesn't rewrite architecture
- limited SDK adjustments that are understood and testable
- packaging changes with a clear rollback and controlled scope

The logic: you need time for at least one stable verification loop, plus time to react if you find regressions.

When to add +2 weeks

Add **+2 weeks** when the change touches **multiple** high-risk areas, or one area with wide blast radius:

- saves/persistence changes
- broad refactors in stability/performance paths
- online changes tied to platform services
- packaging/pipeline changes that alter how content is built or delivered
- SDK integration changes late in the cycle

The logic: you're buying two loops: discovery and correction, not just discovery.

When to stop and re-baseline

You stop pretending the existing plan is valid and you **re-baseline** when any of these is true:

- **Quality/stability trigger:** you cannot produce a stable candidate build long enough to verify (e.g., repeated regressions, unstable build-to-build behavior, "QA can't test because it changes or breaks").
- **Regression trigger:** the last risky change causes cascading breakage and the team is now spending more time chasing fall-out than closing planned work.
- **Uncertainty trigger:** the team cannot confidently explain what the next verification cycle will prove (you're in guess-and-check mode).
- **Schedule reality trigger:** buffers stack up and your planned dates no longer match the verified closure rate.

Re-baseline is not a failure. It's the moment you stop lying to yourself.

Escalation: who must sign off risky console changes (role-based)

For any change that trips the risk triggers above, sign-off is required. Use roles, not titles.

Decider (must exist):

Owns the call and accepts the trade-off (scope/time/quality). The Decider must be explicitly named for the change category (scope, pillars, tech).

Recommender (required):

Brings options, impact, risks, and a recommendation. In console risk scenarios, the recommender should ensure the decision is not made on vibes.

Contributors (required):

Provide input on cost, verification impact, and failure modes. At minimum this should include:

- someone who owns the affected system (tech contributor),
- someone who owns validation reality (QA contributor),

- and where relevant, someone who owns UX/design implications.

Informed (mandatory communication target):

All leads whose area will change as a result, plus anyone responsible for scheduling/build drops.
Hard stop-rule: if a risky change has no named Decider and no verification plan, it does not ship into a console candidate branch/build.

This checklist is conservative on purpose. Console pipelines punish optimism. If you classify risk early and apply buffers before the platform forces you to, you keep control of the schedule instead of reacting to it.

IV. Console Focus: platform constraints as product constraints

PC-first teams often talk about "the console port" like it's a packaging step. As if you take the finished game, recompile it, adjust a few buttons, and ship.

That belief is not optimistic. It's dangerous.

On current-gen consoles, platform constraints don't sit on the side of the project. They shape what the product *is*. If you treat them as "technical problems" to solve later, you'll eventually solve them anyway – just under time pressure, with forced quality compromises, and with the worst kind of rework: the kind that touches design, UX, and feel.

This chapter is about flipping that mindset early. Not because you want to design "for constraints" instead of "for fun," but because constraints define whether the fun can be delivered reliably on the platform you intend to sell.

1) How "platform constraints" become part of the product

Console constraints become product constraints in three ways.

First: consoles enforce a single experience.

On PC, you can absorb a lot of issues through settings, hardware variance, and the player's willingness to tweak. On console, you ship one baseline. The player's expectation is not "let me tune this." It's "this should just work."

That means performance and UX are not adjustable layers. They're part of the promise.

Second: console friction is interpreted as quality.

A menu that hitches, a focus path that gets stuck, a control scheme that fights muscle memory – these are not "small issues." They're immediate signals that the game is not premium, not stable, not trustworthy. Players don't separate "port quality" from "game quality." They just judge the product.

Third: consoles punish late changes with external latency.

You can't treat iteration as infinite. Every attempt costs more time, more verification, more risk, and sometimes external dependency. That reality forces discipline. If you don't build discipline early, the platform will impose it later.

So when you say "platform constraints," what you really mean is: **what kind of product we are allowed to ship.**

2) Performance/controls/UX as hard constraints inside the alignment one-pager

If you already use an alignment one-pager (and you should), the console shift is simple: put platform constraints into the same document as pillars and scope.

Not in a separate "tech doc." Not as tribal knowledge. In the same artifact that defines what wins.

The key is to phrase them as *hard constraints*, not wishes.

Examples of constraints that belong in the one-pager for a PC-first project with planned current-gen console ports:

- **Controls are controller-first compatible:** input mapping must be comfortable, consistent, and remappable where feasible.
- **UI must be couch-usable:** readable at distance, safe-area compliant, predictable focus navigation, no "mouse-first" assumptions.
- **Menu experience must be stable:** "zero jank" expectation – no stutters, missed inputs, broken focus, or long UI lag.
- **Performance and stability are part of "definition of done":** if it's playable on PC but unstable on target console, it's not "done" for a console-bound product.

Those aren't technical notes. They are product boundaries. They should influence prioritization and trade-offs the same way scope and pillars do.

And they should be enforceable through your existing mechanisms:

- changes go through Evaluate -> Decide -> Communicate,
- risky platform changes trigger buffers and sign-off,

- decisions that affect console experience get recorded and communicated.

3) Decisions that MUST account for console from day one

You picked two: input and UI. Good. In action games, these are not peripheral systems. They are the player's hands and eyes.

A) Input decisions: action mapping is game feel

From day one, any decision that changes:

- number of actions required in combat,
- how often the player needs to aim while moving,
- reliance on quick toggles, holds, or chord combinations,
- timing sensitivity (parries, cancels, quick swaps),

...must be evaluated against controller ergonomics and console expectations.

If you design a control scheme that "works" on keyboard but becomes uncomfortable on controller, you don't just have a mapping problem later. You have a combat design problem. You'll either:

- cut actions,
- simplify systems,
- or ship a layout that feels like friction.

All three are design outcomes.

The early win is to treat controller mapping as a design constraint, not a late-stage localization step. That reduces rework and prevents "controller compromises" that blunt the game's identity.

B) UI decisions: focus navigation changes what UI can be

PC UI often gets away with density and precision because the mouse makes it navigable. Console UI is governed by focus paths. That changes what "good UI" even means.

From day one, any decision that changes:

- inventory structure,
- loadout complexity,
- menu depth and cross-linking,
- tutorial flow and settings granularity,

...must be evaluated against focus navigation, couch readability, and the "zero jank" standard in menus.

If you build a PC-first UI architecture that assumes hover, small targets, deep nested panels, and fast mouse travel, you will pay for it later with a redesign – not a reskin.

The early win is to define a console-friendly navigation model and readability baseline early enough that the UI grows inside that box.

4) Anti-pattern: "we'll port later, it'll be fine" – why it backfires

This is one of the most expensive lies teams tell themselves.

It backfires because it encourages you to build systems that are "locally optimal" on PC and globally expensive later.

You'll see it in three places:

Controls: PC design accumulates actions and complexity because it's easy to add one more keybind. Later you realize the controller has hard ergonomic limits. Now you're forced to simplify gameplay, not just remap it.

UI: PC UI becomes dense and mouse-dependent. Later you discover focus navigation makes it painful. Now you're forced to redesign structure and flow, not just increase font size.

Performance/stability: you postpone performance discipline until late, because PC can brute-force more. Later console stability becomes the product gate. Now you downgrade visuals and cut features under pressure, instead of making deliberate trade-offs earlier.

The worst part is that "we'll port later" often isn't a conscious decision. It's just what happens when constraints aren't written down and enforced. The team drifts into a PC-optimized reality and then tries to reverse-engineer console compatibility when time is gone.

That's not a port. That's a rescue.

Rule of thumb summary

If you intend to ship on consoles, treat console constraints as product constraints from day one. Put them into the alignment one-pager next to pillars and scope, and enforce them through your existing decision and change gates. Input and UI are not "port tasks" in action games – they are core design boundaries. And if anyone says "we'll port later, it'll be fine," assume they just volunteered the project for late rework, forced downgrades, and schedule pain.

Table of Content

AFTERWORD

This book is a distillation of what I've seen and learned in game development – patterns that repeat across teams, genres, and production styles. It's based on real experience, not theory.

That also means one important thing: I won't always be right.

Every studio has its own constraints, culture, and failure modes. Some teams need more structure. Some need less. Some problems are solved by process. Others are solved by leadership decisions, hiring, or simply time. What I'm offering here is a practical set of tools that has worked for me and for teams around me – but you should treat it as a starting point, not as a doctrine.

My mission with this series is simple: reduce a bit of the daily friction that makes gamedev unnecessarily stressful. Less chaos. Fewer reopened decisions. Fewer "we'll figure it out later" traps. More projects that ship without burning the team.

If this book helped you – even a little – I'd appreciate a review. Reviews are how books like this stay visible and reach the people who need them. A few honest sentences make a real difference.

This is also the first book in the *Gamedev Anti-Chaos Series*. I'm working on the next volumes already, each focused on a specific slice of production reality: alignment, decision making, momentum, change control, and the places where teams typically lose predictability.

If you want to follow the work as it develops, the easiest way is to follow me on social media and/or reach out directly. I read messages, and I'm interested in what breaks in your projects and what actually helps.

And if you want a more hands-on system – tool you can use day-to-day with your team – I recommend my **Gamedev Production and Design Workbook**. This book gives you the mental model and the operating rules. The workbook gives you a practical companion you can apply in the middle of production, when you don't have time to reinvent structure from scratch.

Thanks for reading. I hope it makes your next project calmer, clearer, and more shippable.

Leszek

AFTERWORD

[illegible]

[illegible]

[illegible]

[illegible]

[illegible]

[illegible]

[illegible]

[illegible]

[illegible]

Made in United States
Orlando, FL
04 November 2026

90202061R00157